S0-BRD-612

Writing in the Schools

Improvement Through Effective Leadership

Allan A. Glatthorn

National Association of Secondary School Principals
Reston, Virginia

ISBN 88210-128-5

Copyright 1981

National Association of Secondary School Principals
1904 Association Dr., Reston, Va. 22091

Contents

Foreword

STUDENT WRITING, until recently, has rarely been the subject of headlines. Unlike reading, science, foreign languages, physical fitness, and others, writing instruction has not been scrutinized by study committees and critics.

Today, however, writing and its importance as an essential lifetime skill are being looked at very closely by both the public and the professional educator. Questions about how writing is taught and what practices are most successful are being posed as the quest for competencies in basic skills continues.

For principals, especially those whose backgrounds are not in English or language arts teaching, providing answers to these kinds of questions is not easy. Yet, as principals they are expected to have answers. They are the instructional leaders in their schools; and students, parents, citizens, and teachers look to them for direction and guidance.

We believe this book by Allan Glatthorn will help principals. *Writing in the Schools—Improvement Through Effective Leadership* is truly written for them. It first describes the writing process in clear, concise language, and then addresses the kinds of considerations that should interest instructional leaders—how to improve writing, how to supervise its instruction, and how to evaluate a writing program. Many books on writing are on the market for teachers; few, if any, are specifically directed at school administrators who have ultimate responsibility for instructional programs.

We commend this book to your serious reading. We believe Allan Glatthorn provides readers with insights to the instruction of writing not available elsewhere under one cover. A bonus is a chapter to assist readers develop more fully their own writing skills.

Thomas F. Koerner

Editorial Director
NASSP

Preface

INTEREST IN THE teaching of writing has increased during the past few years. The concerns of parents, teachers, and administrators have prompted researchers to conduct studies about effective ways to teach writing and the processes students use when they write. A number of articles and books have been published advising teachers how to use that knowledge to improve the quality of student writing.

Little attention has been given, however, to the key role of the school principal in leading an all-school program focused on the teaching of writing. My own experience as a high school principal taught me the importance of my involvement and support of any curriculum improvement effort. And recent research on effective schools indicates beyond reasonable doubt that the principal is a key factor in all school improvement efforts.

This monograph is intended to provide principals the skills they need to lead a schoolwide writing improvement effort. It includes suggestions for steps principals can take, in collaboration with their teachers, to improve student writing.

The monograph begins by reviewing what is known about the composing processes and the teaching of writing in order to establish a knowledge base for what follows. A process is explained which will enable you to assess your school's present writing program. The assessment data can then be used to highlight the need for and give direction to a staff development program.

Several models are presented for the writing curriculum, along with a process for developing the composition curriculum. Considerable space is given to working with English teachers and department heads, the chief agents in effecting improvement in writing ability. But there is now general agreement that the greatest improvement will come about when teachers in every department make writing an important part of the learning experience. Therefore, suggestions are included for some specific ways that principals can lead a schoolwide effort to improve student writing.

Another important concern is how best to supervise an ongoing composition program. Some specific suggestions are made for planning and implementing a collegial effort to monitor and supervise the composition program in both its curricular and instructional aspects.

Many of the new writing instruction programs challenge the conventional wisdom about the teaching of writing. For example, they give less attention to the study of formal grammar and the close correction of papers by the classroom teacher. There is a need to inform parents and community members about such new efforts and to enlist their support for programs that are concerned more with creative expression and clear writing and less with "correctness." Some methods are described that principals can use to meet that need.

The monograph ends with some practical suggestions for improving administrative communication. A principal who values writing, who writes clearly, and who uses the language effectively, will provide an influential role model for both teachers and students.

This monograph is intended to enable secondary school administrators to provide effective leadership in improving the writing of the students in their schools. It clearly will require a collaborative effort—but the principal will provide the best direction.

A.A.G.

Acknowledgments

I WISH TO THANK my colleagues conducting research in the teaching of writing who have so generously shared their findings and their materials. I also feel a special sense of gratitude to those curriculum directors, department heads, and English teachers who provided materials for inclusion in the resource list. And all my professional work is stimulated and supported by my wife, Barbara, who deserves much more than this public acknowledgment of her contribution.

1. The Composing Process and the Teaching of Writing

FOR YEARS WE taught composition primarily by instinct and intuition, operating without the benefit of sound research. Now, however, that situation has changed. We know a great deal about how students write—and what teachers can do to improve student writing. It is useful for you as a school administrator to know that research, so that the programs developed in your school are grounded on a solid foundation of reliable research.

Let us turn first to the composing process. While authorities differ in how they conceptualize the process, they do agree about the following general principles.

- *The composing process is complex, involving memory, cognition, language, and psychomotor behaviors.*

    For younger and unskilled writers especially this complexity results in a cognitive overload: The writer feels tension and anxiety because there is so much to think about, so many decisions to make.

- *The composing process is multiphased, involving several different stages and many subprocesses.*

    While there is no general agreement about the terms used in identifying these stages, there is a consensus about their general nature and order of occurrence. Earlier theorists postulated three stages: prewriting, drafting, and revising. Current researchers, believing that the three-stage model is deceptively simple, offer more sophisticated representations. I have found it useful in my own work to identify five stages: exploring, planning, drafting, revising, and sharing. Figure 1.1 defines these five stages briefly and identifies both the mental activities and observable behaviors that accompany each stage.

- *The process seems recursive and interactive; the stages overlap, relate closely to each other, and affect each other.*

    Earlier models of the composing process were linear. There was an initial prewriting stage, followed by a drafting stage, which in turn was succeeded by a revising stage. Current models, derived from numerous studies of both skilled and unskilled writers, reflect a more complex and interactive process.

1

Figure 1.1

A Model of the Composing Process

Stage	Definition	Mental Activities	Observable Behaviors
Exploring	A series of mental activities and processes used by the writer to examine the external world and explore the internal one, preparatory to making decisions about planning and writing	Sensing a reason to write Considering the subject Thinking about what one knows about the subject Considering voice and tone Considering audience Considering purpose Considering medium Sharpening cognitive processes Discovering divergent approaches Examining beliefs and attitudes Trying out language is sub-vocalization Retrieving additional information	Jotting notes Asking questions Reading, reviewing Discussing ideas
Planning	A series of mental decisions about the content and order of the writing, often translated into written notes and sketches	Choosing subject Selecting ideas, information to be included Deciding about order	Making notes Making diagrams Making sketches Making outlines

Drafting	A series of psychomotor behaviors (drawing, writing, typing) by which words and sentences are written	Deciding about general form Deciding about voice, tone, medium Choosing beginning strategy Searching for words Trying out pieces of sentences Thinking about paragraph shape	Talking about choices Mumbling Writing phrases and sentences
Revising	A series of decisions to change and rearrange what has been written	Reading what has been written Looking for errors Rethinking choices Trying out other words and sentence forms Trying out other arrangements and orders	Crossing out Adding parts Rearranging parts Correcting errors Changing words Reading aloud
Sharing	A series of exchanges with individuals in which both the ideas and the writing are shared	Deciding to share Deciding what is to be shared Deciding on medium of sharing	Discussing Reading aloud Exchanging papers Posting Publishing

Figure 1.2
A Model of the Composing Process

Exploring

Planning

Drafting

Revising

Sharing

As Figure 1.2 suggests, there is a great deal of overlap in the five stages. Exploring continues well into the drafting stage. Planning occurs before and during the drafting stage. Revising begins almost as soon as the drafting is started. And the sharing process continues throughout the other four stages.

The process is also interactive, as the diagram suggests. The planning decisions open up new avenues of exploration; the act of writing impinges upon both the exploring and the planning; the sharing provides data for planning, drafting, and revising.

The model is useful in describing how most of us write when we have sufficient time. However, we differ a great deal in its use when we are involved in a particular composing task. If we know a great deal about a topic the exploring stage is abbreviated. If we are logical in our approach to writing the planning may be almost automatic. If we are skilled writers, composing under the pressure of deadlines, there may be little revising. If we write in a private journal there is no sharing. The model represents a general conceptualization of how we compose under optimum conditions; it is not a formula for solving a particular writing problem.

In fact, we now have a significant body of evidence which reveals that skilled and unskilled writers differ markedly in the way they compose. Figure 1.3 summarizes the important differences identified in several reliable investigations of the composing processes. Note that the unskilled writer, unlike the skilled composer, makes only minimal use of plans and revises in a perfunctory manner. This difference seems clearly related to the quality of the writing produced.

Findings about the composing process have some clear and important implications for the teaching of writing. First, teachers should make students aware of the composing processes they currently use and the extent to which those processes might be counterproductive. One way to accomplish this goal is to use a self-assessment form. An example is shown in Figure 1.4. Teachers who have used the form report that it is useful in helping students think about their own composing processes.

4

Figure 1.3
The Composing Processes of Unskilled and Skilled Writers

Stage	Unskilled Writers	Skilled Writers
Exploring	Do not consider exploring important or useful	Consider exploring activities useful and helpful
	Spend little time exploring	Spend more time considering and contemplating
Planning	Typically make no plans before they write	Accompany their planning with note-taking, sketching, diagramming
	Prefer not to outline; make outlines after piece is drafted	
	Develop limited plans as they write	
Drafting	Write in a way that imitates speech	Write in a way that is less like speech
	Write without concern for reader	Show more sensitivity to reader
	Are preoccupied with technical matters of spelling and punctuation	Spend more time in drafting
	Do not pause very much	Frequently stop to rescan, reread, reflect
	Do not rescan or reflect	Respond to all aspects of rhetorical problem—audience, medium, voice, etc.
	Focus on topic alone, not the whole rhetorical problem	
Revising	Either revise very little or only at the surface and word levels	Either revise very little or revise extensively at sentence and paragraph level
	See revision mainly as "error hunting"	Are more concerned with content and reader appeal
	Stop revising when they feel they have not violated any rules	Do not become unduly concerned with matters of form
	Spend so much time and energy on changing spelling and punctuation during drafting stage that they lose sight of larger problems	See revising as recursive and ongoing
	Often see revising as "making a neat copy in ink"	

5

Sharing	Are often reluctant to share writing	Are usually eager to share
	Share in order to receive reassurance	Share in order to receive constructive feedback
		See publishing and dissemination of writing as important

(The picture presented above is a composite drawn from the following studies of the composing processes of skilled and unskilled writers: Stallard, 1974; Mischel, 1974; Graves, 1975; Sawkins, 1975; Sommers, 1980; Crowley, 1976; Metzger, 1976; Bechtel, 1979; Perl, 1979; Pianko, 1979.)

Second, teachers should help students deal with the complexities of the composing process by "fractionating" and "routinizing." The teacher can fractionate the composing process by helping students deal with one stage at a time, thus simplifying the task of writing. The teacher can help students explore and then plan, helping them to use specific steps at each stage. The teacher can routinize the composing process by helping students develop a series of schemes and strategies for handling some recurring problems.

For example, the teacher can show students how to use a routine to plan an expository process essay: "Tell the steps in the process in the order in which they should occur." This fractionating and routinizing will reduce the cognitive demands of writing, enabling students to deal with more important issues of content and language.

Third, teachers should slow down the entire composing process. Unskilled writers tend to be impulsive. They see writing as an unpleasant chore to be completed with dispatch and rush through the process without sufficient reflection. Too often teachers reinforce these "hurry up and finish" behaviors by making assignments without providing time for the processes and by setting close deadlines without giving the students time to use the processes.

The final recommendation grows out of the preceding three suggestions: Teachers should emphasize the exploring, planning, revising, and sharing processes so that students develop the requisite skills and gain the benefits of these critical stages.

Some Generalizations

6

These findings about the composing process and their implications for teaching are reinforced and supported by a significant body of research related to the teaching of writing. The generalizations about the teaching of writing which are discussed below are not the outcomes of one or two unreplicated studies; they are the conclusions reached by numerous researchers following well-designed and carefully conducted studies.

- *The study of formal grammar is not related to improvement in writing and may in fact take time away from the teaching of writing.*
Although there are still some members of the profession who defend

Figure 1.4
Evaluating Your Writing: Attitudes, Practices, and Processes

Good writers use these attitudes, practices and processes. Do you?

Attitudes
1. Value writing as a way of knowing and communicating. _____
2. Respond positively to assigned topics and deadlines. _____

Practices
3. Create for themselves a good writing environment. _____
4. Write frequently on their own in a journal or notebook. _____

Processes
5. Explore a topic and collect information, considering message, audience, and tone—and continue to explore as they write. _____
6. Plan their writing before they start and continue to plan as they write. _____
7. Write rough drafts without giving too much attention to minor matters of form, but give continuing attention to exploration and planning. _____
8. As they write, revise by considering larger issues of emphasis, meaning, and organization. _____
9. Share their writing with friends and editors, inviting their responses and suggestions. _____
10. Continue to revise by polishing the draft, checking sentence structure, spelling, punctuation, usage, and word choice. _____
11. Try to publish what they have written, taking care that the published draft is free of errors. _____

the teaching of grammar as a way to improve writing (see, for example, Newkirk, 1978), most researchers and theorists are convinced that the study of the parts of speech and the parts of the sentence will not help students write better. Abrahamson (1977) is one of several investigators who reached that conclusion after reviewing decades of research on the issue. The study of grammar can be defended on other grounds —but it will not improve student writing.

- *Sentence combining practice will help students write sentences that are more syntactically mature.*

Many studies conducted during the past decade have concluded that giving students directed practice in combining short, simple sentences will help them write longer and more mature sentences. (See, for example, Sandra Stotsky's (1975) excellent review of several sentence combining studies.) Sentence combining activities tend to be of two sorts: signaled and open. Here is an example of a signaled activity, in which the student is given a cue:

Combine the two sentences in the way suggested.
John noticed SOMETHING.
His brother seemed depressed. (THAT)
(Result: John noticed that his brother seemed depressed.)

In an open activity, no cue or signal is provided:

Combine the following short sentences into one longer one:
Students will write better.
They will use all the steps.
These steps are part of the composing process.
They will take more time for prewriting and revising.
(Result: Students who use all the steps in the composing process will write better because they will take more time for prewriting and revising.)

Notice that neither the signaled nor the open exercise makes use of any grammatical terminology.

- *Frequency of writing in and of itself is not associated with improvement in writing.*
This finding is one that most administrators and teachers find difficult to accept, since it seems logical at first glance to assume that more writing will result in better writing. But writing is not a natural skill that develops simply through additional practice. It is instead a complex art which requires coaching and guided practice if it is to be mastered. Teachers who assign and grade a theme every week are not going to bring about much improvement in writing. Haynes' summary of the research is so appropriate that it warrants quoting:

Teachers should give greater emphasis to the guiding and careful development of a limited number of papers, with attention given to direct methods of instruction and to the solving of communication problems before and during the writing process, rather than on the hurried production of a greater number of papers.*

- *A relationship exists between increased reading and improved writing.*
Several studies (see Haynes' 1978 review) suggest that students who read widely learn to write better. It seems quite likely that reading good writing helps us internalize a great deal of knowledge about words, sentences, and paragraphs.

- *Prewriting experiences (which I call "exploring and planning" activities) help students learn to write better.*
Several reviews (see Petrosky, 1974, for example) have concluded that such prewriting activities as role-playing, discussing, reading,

8

---

*E. F. Haynes, "Using Research in Preparing To Teach Writing," *English Journal* 67 (1978): 87.

brainstorming, using metaphors and analogies, and meditating will result in both more divergent content and more effective communication. Those exploring and planning activities help the student sense a reason for writing, consider the audience, broaden the knowledge base, explore the topic, and clarify matters of organization.

- *Peer feedback and peer editing can effect improvements in writing.*

Wolter's and Lamberg's (1976) summary of the research on feedback agrees with similar reviews that peer feedback can be useful in helping students identify problems in their writing and discover ways to remedy those problems. There is some tentative evidence that such feedback will be more effective if it is carefully structured; teachers should show students how to review, edit, and respond to each other's writing.

- *The type or intensity of teacher evaluation is not related to the improvement of writing.*

This finding also challenges the conventional wisdom that teachers should correct and grade all papers very carefully. The evidence suggests that, while students need feedback about their writing, heavy use of the red pencil does not help students write better. (See Bamberg, 1978, for a review of the research on teacher grading.)

- *There is no significant difference between the effects of positive or negative teacher criticism of student writing.*

Positive criticism, however, is more effective in promoting desirable attitudes toward writing. Although most teachers believe that negative criticism should be avoided, VanDeWeghe's (1978) review of research does not support such a position. While excessively negative criticism is likely to produce a negative attitude toward writing, some kind of corrective and constructive feedback is probably essential.

- *While there does not seem to be any evidence to support one revision process over another, there is substantial evidence that revision is critical in improving writing. (Bamberg, 1978.)*

Students who learn how to revise and who are required to revise learn to write better than those who do not.

These findings about the composing process and the development of writing ability are neither definitive nor final. Writing is a highly complex skill that is developed in subtle and often imperceptible ways. Continued research on composing will undoubtedly produce additional insight about theoretical and pedagogical issues. For the time being, however, the generalizations discussed above can provide reliable guidance to school administrators and teachers in evaluating programs and in planning for their improvement.

9

2. Evaluating Your School's Writing Program

A CAREFUL ASSESSMENT is the first step in improving your school's writing program. The extent of that assessment will depend, of course, on the resources available to you and the degree to which your school is involved in state or district programs for assessing writing achievement. The following discussion will give you some suggestions for conducting your own assessment or for extending a state or district evaluation.

The first step is to determine whether there is sufficient support for the writing program at the district and school levels. Too often the school administrator begins by evaluating English teachers, ignoring the obvious fact that writing programs will flourish best when they enjoy strong support from district administrators, school administrators, and the entire faculty.

In making such an assessment you should find a form like that shown in Figure 2.1 a useful tool. Note that the form considers in turn the support provided by district administrators, school administrators, and teachers in other departments. Another useful form for school administrators has been developed by Stephen M. Koziol, Jr., for the Pennsylvania Department of Education (Koziol, 1981).

You can use such a form in a variety of ways. You can use it to make your own objective assessment. An assessment task force, if one exists, can use it in making its evaluations. You might wish to distribute it at a general faculty meeting, have all teachers complete it, and then discuss its results at a later session. It would seem most important, however, to have the English teachers complete the form, since they are typically held most responsible for improving student writing.

The next level of assessment to be made is with the English department in general. Your objective here is to provide the leadership necessary to help the department examine its own commitment and support for the writing program. The criteria listed in Figure 2.2 can be used in two ways. First, the English teachers themselves should make their own assessments. Second, district supervisors and school administrators familiar with the English program can record their evaluations. The results of those two assessments can be used to identify areas where additional study is needed and areas where improvement is indicated.

11

Figure 2.1
Assessing District and Schoolwide Support
for Writing

Criteria	Response		
	Yes	?	No
1. Does the district provide sufficient time and money for inservice programs related to the teaching of writing?	___	___	___
2. Does the district provide sufficient funds for the purchase of instructional materials that teachers need to improve student writing?	___	___	___
3. Does the district provide sufficient funds to support student newspapers and student magazines?	___	___	___
4. Does the district have a written statement of policy governing the content and dissemination of both schoolwide and classroom publications?	___	___	___
5. Does the school make systematic efforts to inform parents about its writing program and to solicit parent involvement in the improvement of that program?	___	___	___
6. Do school administrators write frequently and share their writing with members of the staff?	___	___	___
7. Do school administrators support the requests of teachers to attend conferences and professional meetings concerned with the teaching of writing?	___	___	___
8. Do school administrators encourage teachers to arrange programs in which professional writers and others who use writing in their careers speak to students about writing; and do administrators provide time and funds for such programs?	___	___	___
9. Does the school help teachers, students, and parents value the importance of writing by displaying student writing and providing suitable recognition for excellent student writers?	___	___	___
10. Do school administrators encourage teachers to publish classroom newspapers and magazines and to make other suitable arrangements for the informal dissemination of student writing?	___	___	___
11. Do school administrators encourage all teachers (not just English teachers) to be responsible for developing student writing abilities and to cooperate in			

establishing schoolwide programs for
improving student writing?   ___ ___ ___

12. Do teachers in all the academic disciplines
require students to write, both as a way of
learning and as a way of assessing
learning?   ___ ___ ___

What aspects of the district or schoolwide support for the teaching
of writing deserve special commendation?

1. _____
2. _____
3. _____

What aspects of the district or schoolwide support for the teaching of writing require greatest improvement?

1. _____
2. _____
3. _____

If you require additional information about English teacher attitudes
toward the teaching of writing, you might wish to use one of the instruments cited in the resource list on page 83.

This general assessment of the English department can be supple-
mented if you wish by observations of individual teachers. Chapter 6
includes some specific suggestions about making such observations once
a new program has been instituted. Such observations can also be used
as part of the initial assessment.

The most important aspect of the assessment program, of course, is
the evaluation of student achievement. Here you cannot rely on stan-
dardized tests. Cooper (1975, p. 117) notes:

> Standardized, multiple-choice tests of "writing" like the EST-published
> STEP Writing test and the writing section in the Scholastic Aptitude Test
> may be good predictors of success in school and college English courses...
> but they are inappropriate as writing achievement or performance or growth
> measures. They obviously lack face, content, and construct validity.

A direct measure of writing ability is needed if you want to find out
how well students can write. There are essentially two evaluation
processes available to your teachers: holistic scoring and primary trait
analysis. When teachers use a holistic scoring process to evaluate student writing, they read the paper for its overall quality, forming a general impression of its value. While they are undoubtedly influenced by
specific characteristics of the paper such as sentence structure or paragraph development, they do not explicitly weigh such features. Nor
do they determine in advance what features are important.

Holistic scoring is both efficient and reliable. Trained readers can
read up to 40 papers an hour. And, according to Diederich (1974),
inter-rater reliability of holistic scoring is about .60 to .80. Holistic
scoring is most useful for providing an accurate picture of a student's
ability to write; it does not, however, yield specific information about
the strengths and weaknesses of the writing.

13

Figure 2.2
Assessing the English Department's Commitment to the Teaching of Writing

Criteria	Response		
	Yes	?	No

1. Is there general agreement among the English teachers about the importance of writing and the need to make it an important part of the English curriculum? ___ ___ ___

2. Is there a recently published or revised composition curriculum guide, and was that guide developed with substantial input by English teachers? ___ ___ ___

3. Have all English teachers had recent and systematic inservice training in the teaching of writing? ___ ___ ___

4. Has the English department developed and implemented procedures for keeping and sharing cumulative records of student writing? ___ ___ ___

5. Does the English department provide time in its departmental meetings for continuing discussion of issues related to the teaching of writing? ___ ___ ___

6. Does the English department, in cooperation with school administration, conduct systematic assessments of student writing, and are the results of those assessments used in improving the writing program? ___ ___ ___

What aspects of the English department's commitment to the teaching of writing deserve special commendation?
1. _____
2. _____

What aspects of the English department's commitment to teaching of writing require greatest improvement?
1. _____
2. _____

Specific information results from the use of primary trait analysis. After the teachers have determined the assignment they will use to measure student writing, they identify the primary traits of a piece that responds successfully to the assignment. Those traits become the criteria for scoring the papers. Here, for example, are the criteria used by the National Assessment of Educational Progress in scoring papers where students were asked to write their principal a letter explaining their solution to a school problem:

Rating	*Criteria*
1	Respondents do not identify a problem or give no evidence that the problem can be solved or is worth solving.
2	Respondents identify a problem and either tell how to solve it *or* tell how the school would be improved if it were solved.
3	Respondents identify a problem, explain how to solve the problem, *and* tell how the school would be improved if the problem were solved.
4	Respondents include the elements of a "3" paper. In addition, the elements are expanded and presented in a systematic structure that reflects the steps necessary to solve the problem. (Mullis, 1974)

The primary trait evaluation method yields more specific information about student achievement. It also is more time-consuming and expensive. For this reason many experts recommend that holistic scoring be used for larger samples and primary trait analysis for smaller groups.

Hendrickson (1980) describes a districtwide assessment process that successfully combines both methods: The assessors in the Eugene, Oreg., school district first made a holistic assessment of the writing of 500 sixth graders selected at random from the school's population. Each piece of writing was read by two raters, who assigned a score of 1, 2, 3, or 4. The student's final score was the average of the two ratings. Elementary teachers were asked to identify the skills or traits which should have been used in those exercises, and the papers were analyzed to determine whether these specific skills had been mastered. These two analyses enabled the district to give each elementary and secondary principal a computer printout showing the results for each school, indicating position according to districtwide achievement, and noting specific writing problems needing attention.

In brief, if you wish to make a general assessment of the writing achievement of all students in your school and have limited resources, you should probably use a holistic assessment process. The steps that should be taken are outlined below. Before beginning, however, the English department head should receive special training in conducting such an assessment or should read carefully the very helpful and detailed explanation found in Miles Myers' monograph, *A Procedure for Writing Assessment and Holistic Scoring.**

15

First, a committee of teachers should decide what kind of writing should be assessed. Most assessment programs ask students to write one or more of the following: a business letter, an explanation, a description or report, an argumentation. They then develop the "prompt," the statement explaining the type of writing and the topic. Here is one prompt that Myers reports has been successful in the Oakland, Calif., assessment program:

---

*M. Meyers, *A Procedure for Writing Assessment and Holistic Scoring* (Urbana, Ill.: National Council of Teachers of English, 1980).

1. Describe one thing you would change about school and one thing you would not change about school. Tell why you would change it or why you would not change it.

Two prompts for each type of writing are probably required: one for the morning classes and one for the afternoon classes. In this way students who took the test in the morning will not be able to discuss the topic at lunch with those taking the test in the afternoon. The prompts should be field-tested by having a few students and teachers try them. Detailed directions for administering the writing test are then prepared for the teachers.

On the day the test is administered, each student fills out a file card on which he or she puts the usual identifying information, along with a code number; the student then uses that code number instead of a name on the paper itself. In this way the classroom teachers, but not the raters, know who wrote each paper. The students then write in response to the prompts that have been provided; for secondary students a class period is usually sufficient time for the teacher to give directions and for the students to write.

The scoring then begins. Experienced teachers are asked to assemble in a "scoring room" to review procedures, develop the rating system, and read the papers. They first decide how many rating categories they will use; Myers recommends six as being suitable for most purposes. The readers are then asked to read for an hour to select the "anchor papers" for each category. The anchor papers are the ones representative of a given score; they will be used to guide the systematic rating which will follow. They are read by all the raters and the scores are tallied. The anchor papers which receive the most consistent grades are then used as the "official anchors" in the rating process.

The head reader uses the anchor papers to train all those who will be doing the reading. Each paper receives two ratings. If the two scores differ by more than one point a third reading is recommended.

The results of the assessment should be systematized and analyzed in a final report prepared for teachers, administrators, and parents. The final report should include the prompt, the scores (with an explanation of each), a chart showing the grade-by-grade distribution of scores, an analysis of the strengths and weaknesses evident in the samples, and recommendations for teachers and administrators.

16

Two other kinds of measures can be used to assess student attitude and perceptions. First, you and your teachers may decide to measure student attitudes toward writing. If so, you should consider using either of two well-validated instruments: the Emig-King Written Attitude Scale for Students (1979), or the Daly-Miller Writing Anxiety Scale (1975). As perhaps is suggested by their titles, the Emig-King measure is the more general of the two. While the Daly-Miller instrument is concerned primarily with anxiety and apprehension about writing, the Emig-King instrument assesses three categories: preference for writing, perception of writing, and process of writing.

Figure 2.3
Student Perception of Writing Instruction

Directions: Below are several statements about how writing is taught in the English classroom. Read each statement carefully. Then decide how often that statement applies to your English class. Circle your answer.

1. The writing I do for English class seems useful to me.	Almost Always	Often	Sometimes	Seldom	Almost Never
2. In our English class we can choose the topics we write about.	Almost Always	Often	Sometimes	Seldom	Almost Never
3. My English teacher writes when we are asked to write.	Almost Always	Often	Sometimes	Seldom	Almost Never
4. My English teacher encourages me to revise my writing.	Almost Always	Often	Sometimes	Seldom	Almost Never
5. When I write for English class, I am given enough time to think about the topic and get the information I need.	Almost Always	Often	Sometimes	Seldom	Almost Never
6. When preparing to write in English class, I am able to discuss ideas with my classmates.	Almost Always	Often	Sometimes	Seldom	Almost Never
7. My English teacher gives me helpful criticism about the writing I have done.	Almost Always	Often	Sometimes	Seldom	Almost Never
8. My English teacher praises me when I have written a good essay.	Almost Always	Often	Sometimes	Seldom	Almost Never
9. My English teacher teaches us the skills we need to make our papers better.	Almost Always	Often	Sometimes	Seldom	Almost Never
10. In our English class we publish what we have written in classroom newspapers and magazines.	Almost Always	Often	Sometimes	Seldom	Almost Never

17

The other kind of assessment of student perception involves using an instrument similar to the one shown in Figure 2.3. The instrument is intended primarily for use by the classroom teacher who wants to assess student perception about writing instruction in the English class. Since it has not been systematically checked for validity and reliability it should be used only for making informal assessments of student attitudes toward instruction, not for evaluating teachers.

3. Planning and Implementing a Staff Development Program

IF THE SEVERAL assessments explained in the previous chapter have persuaded you and the English department staff that systematic improvement is needed, then the next step should be to plan an inservice program that will develop the skills teachers need to effect such improvement. This chapter explains the steps that should be taken in planning and implementing such a staff development program.

At the outset, let me explain why we should begin with staff development and not curriculum improvement. In so doing, we will almost immediately begin to affect the teacher's performance. If we can help the teachers become more knowledgeable about writing and more skilled in teaching composition, students will begin to profit directly. Further, an effective staff development program can lead to an improved curriculum, as informed teachers exchange ideas, think about issues in the teaching of writing, and make joint decisions about content.

If, on the other hand, we start by asking a committee of teachers to write a curriculum guide, we have no assurance that their work will be based on the best current knowledge about the teaching of writing; nor is it likely that their decisions will reflect the best practice of the rest of the staff.

What role should the administrator play in developing such an inservice program? While your decision will be affected by your leadership style and your sense of priorities, some research can guide you. A four-year study of approximately 300 innovative programs conducted by the Rand Corporation (Berman and McLaughlin, 1978) indicated that an important ingredient of successful inservice was active participation by the principal. But both the Rand study and other recent research (Joyce and Showers, 1980) concluded that the most successful projects were jointly managed by administrators and teachers.

The recommendation, therefore, is clear: Be an active participant in the program but do not dominate it; work cooperatively with teachers in planning and carrying it out. The approach you take will depend upon your local circumstances. A small task force composed of a department head, a few key teachers, and an administrator would probably be effective.

Figure 3.1
Recommendations for Staff Development Programs Derived from Reviews of Research

Duration:
1. The program should be ongoing and continuous.

Management:
1. The principal should participate actively but not dominate.
2. Teachers and administrators should plan the program jointly.
3. There should be regular project meetings in which participants review progress and discuss substantive concerns.

Content:
1. The program should provide a necessary theoretical base for the new skills.
2. The program should give primary attention to the specific skills teachers believe they need.
3. The content should be timely, directly related to immediate job needs.

Learning Activities:
1. The program should make extensive use of hands-on activities and demonstrations of the new skills.
2. The program should provide for the trial of those new skills in simulated or real settings.
3. The program should make it possible for teachers to get structured feedback about their use of those new skills.
4. The program should provide opportunities for observation in other classrooms and districts.

Site:
1. The program should be school-based, not university-based.

Instructors:
1. Local teachers should be the instructors; the program should make maximum use of teachers teaching each other and minimal use of outside consultants.

20

The first thing the task force should do is review the research on effective staff development. Figure 3.1 presents a summary of the characteristics of effective inservice programs, derived from three comprehensive and systematic reviews of the field (Berman and McLaughlin, 1978; Lawrence, 1974; and Joyce and Showers, 1980). These characteristics may suggest the kind of inservice program that will be most successful in your school.

A second knowledge-building task for the committee is to review what is known about adult learners, since the teachers in the inservice

Figure 3.2
Generalizations About Adult Learning That Affect Staff Development

1. Adult needs and interests should be the starting point for developing and organizing adult learning experiences.

2. The most appropriate basis for organizing adult learning is the life situations of those adults, not academic disciplines.

3. The essential methodology in adult learning is the analysis of their experience.

4. The need for adults to be self-directing requires a teacher who can foster mutual inquiry, not simply present new knowledge.

5. Programs for adult learners should take cognizance of the fact that individual differences increase with age.

6. Administrators who expect adults to play new roles should make clear those new role expectations in order to facilitate adult learning.

7. The adult learner needs help in achieving a synthesis of personal goals and organizational expectations.

8. Adult learners need an opportunity to practice and receive feedback about new skills in a supportive and collaborative environment.

program will be playing that role. While we have less empirical research about adult learning styles, we do have some findings and some strong recommendations from the experts. The recommendations shown in Figure 3.2 are derived from some recent work by Knowles (1978) and Klopf (1979).

Note how the generalizations about adult learning reinforce the findings about effective inservice programs. Those two sets of findings considered together provide a sound knowledge base for those responsible for developing any inservice program; in a sense, they describe what might be termed the "ideal" staff development program.

But it is not enough to describe the ideal; school systems are limited by the real constraints of budget, time, and contracts. It is therefore essential for the task force to assess those constraints and identify available resources. They should systematically consider these questions:

21

Constraints

● Have the school board and superintendent set any deadlines by which staff development and curriculum improvement should be completed?

● Does the teachers' contract place any limitations on the timing and funding of staff development?

● What other noninstructional demands placed upon teachers will limit the time, energy, and attention they can devote to the inservice program?

Figure 3.3
Conceptual Levels of Adult Learners and Their Implications for Staff Development

Conceptual Level	General Characteristics	Staff Development Needs and Preferences
Level 1	Respect authority as source of new ideas Concerned with group norms and their applications Skeptical of new ideas Somewhat defensive; threatened by change See others as similar with respect to norms Tend to view everything as it relates to their specific situation	Prefer highly structured, well-organized programs Prefer practical programs: how to do it, when Find it difficult to use broad philosophical system Have difficulty identifying areas where they need help Want authorities who can present new knowledge and show how it applies to their situation Need support in trying out new ideas Want to learn how to use materials in real-life settings Can learn from lectures followed by discussions focusing on application Deal better with limited options
Transition to Level 2	Begin to question group norms Recognize that norms often conflict or do not apply Begin to recognize individual differences in appropriateness of conduct Are concerned with articulating ways in which they differ from the norms	Resist mandatory inservice More concerned with raising questions and clarifying thinking Need support in raising questions Prefer options in program content and activities Prefer group discussion to lectures Can profit from discussions that deal with issues involving disparate points of view Need both individual and group activities

Figure 3.4
Survey of Preferences for Program Design and Structure

Directions: Listed below are features that might characterize our inservice program. Indicate your preferences for each feature by circling one of these symbols:

SA—I *strongly agree* that this feature should characterize our inservice program

A—I *agree* that this feature should characterize our inservice program

?—I am *uncertain* about this feature

D—I *disagree* that this feature should characterize our inservice program

SD—I *strongly disagree* that this feature should characterize our inservice program

1. The inservice program follows a regular schedule with a well-organized agenda for each meeting.   SA A ? D SD

2. The program emphasizes learning practical skills that teachers use in their teaching.   SA A ? D SD

3. The program uses consultants from the outside who are considered experts in the field.   SA A ? D SD

4. The program gives appropriate attention to theory and research.   SA A ? D SD

5. The program enables participants to develop and exchange classroom materials. SA A ? D SD

6. The program makes use of lectures followed by discussions and questions.   SA A ? D SD

7. The program gives participants a chance to discuss controversial issues in the teaching of writing.   SA A ? D SD

8. The program gives participants an option about what they learn and how they learn it.   SA A ? D SD

9. The program emphasizes "hands-on" activities.   SA S ? D SD

10. The program uses local teachers as the instructors, and teachers have much chance to learn from each other.   SA A ? D SD

11. The program provides participants with an opportunity to see new skills demonstrated and practice those skills themselves.   SA A ? D SD

12. The program provides opportunities for observing other classes and schools.   SA A ? D SD

13. The program provides opportunities for participants to try out new skills in their classrooms and get feedback about their use of those skills.   SA A ? D SD

23

Resources

- What school district funds are likely to be available to support the inservice program?
- What outside funding might be available?
- Which members of the faculty can be used as instructional resources?
- What outside consultants are available to assist? What are their areas of expertise?
- What published materials are available to support the inservice program?
- What time is available? Can scheduled inservice days and faculty meetings be used for the staff development program? Can before-school time be used?

That systematic assessment of constraints and resources should enable the task force to determine the general limits of the project. At this juncture the task force should be ready to involve the faculty in actively planning the details of the program. The first concern is to assess the teachers' preferences about the general structure and design of the staff development program. While the general findings cited above are useful in understanding what most teachers prefer, those who have conducted inservice programs know that teachers differ in the kinds of programs they want.

Some recent work by Toni Santmire (1979) supports and clarifies this perception. Santmire draws upon the Conceptual Systems Theory of David Hunt (1966) in identifying the general conceptual framework and inservice needs of faculty. According to Santmire, most adult learners can be classified as either "Level 1" or "Transition to Level 2" learners, with very different learning styles and growth preferences.

The summary in Figure 3.3 is derived from Santmire's work. While I do not think that school principals should classify individual teachers as "Level 1" or "Transition to Level 2" learners, we should try to assess and respond to these individual differences wherever feasible. A survey form like the one shown in Figure 3.4 can be useful in surveying preferences about design and structure.

The second type of assessment concerns the content of the program. Here we have three options. One choice is to use an open-ended questionnaire of the sort recommended by Newlove and Hall (1976):

24

> When you think about our new composition program, what are you concerned about? (Do not say what you think others are concerned about, but only what concerns you.) Please write in complete sentences and please be frank.

These writers offer some helpful suggestions for analyzing the expressed concerns about the change.

Those who wish to make a more systematic analysis of teachers' concerns should also consider using Hall, George, and Rutherford's (1977) "Stages of Concern" questionnaire. The questionnaire takes

Figure 3.5
Survey of Preferences for Program Content

Directions: Listed below are the topics and activities that are often included in inservice programs related to the teaching of writing. Indicate your preferences for each kind of content and activity by circling one of these symbols:

SA—I *strongly agree* that this content or activity should be included

A—I *agree* that this content or activity should be included

?—I am *uncertain* as to whether or not this content or activity should be included

D—I *disagree* that this content or activity should be included

SD—I *strongly disagree* that this content or activity should be included

1. Understanding the composing process and its implications for teaching   SA A ? D SD

2. Developing a composition curriculum for our school   SA A ? D SD

3. Knowing and applying research in the teaching of writing   SA A ? D SD

4. Developing composition assignments   SA A ? D SD

5. Motivating students to write   SA A ? D SD

6. Using prewriting activities to improve student writing   SA A ? D SD

7. Helping students learn to revise   SA A ? D SD

8. Developing sentence-combining materials   SA A ? D SD

9. Using holistic assessment to make schoolwide evaluations of student writing   SA A ? D SD

10. Grading and responding to student writing   SA A ? D SD

11. Using peer conferences to improve writing   SA A ? D SD

12. Implementing a naturalistic or "writer's workshop" approach to student writing   SA A ? D SD

13. Publishing and sharing student writing   SA A ? D SD

14. Doing our own writing and sharing our writing with each other   SA A ? D SD

15. Teaching specific writing skills   SA A ? D SD

16. Facilitating creative writing   SA A ? D SD

17. Relating the study of grammar to the development of writing skills   SA A ? D SD

18. Helping less able students improve their writing   SA A ? D SD

19. Improving writing in other school subjects   SA A ? D SD

20. Working with parents to improve student writing   SA A ? D SD

Other: (Please list any other content you believe should be included)

Figure 3.6
Staff Development Assessment Survey

Directions: Below are several statements about our composition staff development program. Indicate to what extent you agree with each statement by circling one of these symbols:

SA—strongly agree
A—agree
?—uncertain
D—disagree
SD—strongly disagree

1. The staff development program helped me improve my own writing. SA A ? D SD

2. As a result of the staff development program, I feel more confident in my ability to teach writing. SA A ? D SD

3. I believe my students are writing better because I participated in the staff development program. SA A ? D SD

4. The staff development program helped me become a more effective teacher of writing. SA A ? D SD

5. The staff development program helped me become better informed about current theory and research about the teaching of writing. SA A ? D SD

6. The staff development program gave me some good ideas for improving our composition curriculum. SA A ? D SD

7. The staff development program enabled me to work effectively with my colleagues on problems we share. SA A ? D SD

only 15 minutes to administer, can be scored by hand, and gives administrators a clear picture of the kinds of concerns teachers are feeling about the proposed program.

A second choice is to use a structured survey form similar to that shown in Figure 3.5, which lists the topics that might be usefully dealt with in a composition inservice program. Note that the list includes "doing our own writing and sharing our writing with each other." The developers of the National Writing Project, a highly successful program that has centers all across the nation, believe such writing and sharing to be an important component of inservice programs in the teaching of writing.

A third option is to make use of structured interviews and open-ended discussions as ways of eliciting teachers' concerns. Jones and Hayes (1980) remind us that needs assessment surveys are not always valid indicators of true needs; therefore, you and the task force might wish to rely more on interview data and your own observations.

A review of the data will enable you and your task force to plan an inservice program that will meet the needs of the staff and respond to their expressed preferences. Once the program begins, you should, if at all possible, participate actively. Such participation will demonstrate your own commitment to the program and will enable you to become better informed about writing and your teachers' approach to it.

It is important to evaluate the staff development program. The task force should probably be responsible for both the formative and the summative evaluations. Someone on the task force should be responsible for keeping a log of the inservice meetings, noting the topic, the activities, the attendance, and the key presenters.

In addition, members of the task force should assist in accumulating other formative data by interviewing participants, observing reactions during the meeting, and from time to time distributing brief evaluation questionnaires. These formative data can suggest which adjustments are needed to make the inservice sessions more profitable.

The extensiveness of the summative evaluation will depend on the scope of the project, the resources available, and the requirements of the school board or other funding agency. Duke and Corno (1981) describe a comprehensive system for evaluating staff development programs that can be used when a systematic evaluation is required and special resources are available.

A less comprehensive but still useful evaluation could be made by examining the results of the holistic assessments conducted during the first year of the project and those obtained in succeeding years. If such comparisons are not possible, then at the least you might consider using an attitude survey similar to that shown in Figure 3.6. The results will give you a general measure of teacher satisfaction.

With the staff development phase concluded, the teachers should now be ready to turn to the issue of curriculum development, the subject of the next chapter.

4. Improving the Composition Curriculum

It is usually wise to carry out a staff development program before undertaking a curriculum improvement project. However, even if it is not feasible to provide inservice education, it still seems desirable to develop an articulated composition curriculum. In many cases, of course, such a project will be designed and implemented at the district level for all levels of schooling. In this chapter, however, I would like to describe a process that you can use to provide leadership in improving your school's curriculum. You should find the same procedures useful if you are part of a districtwide team.

The leadership you provide can take many forms. You may decide to become very actively involved, assuming a direct leadership role. Or, you may decide to delegate that responsibility to a department head, team leader, or administrative assistant. You may determine that it is best to work through an existing departmental structure, or you may choose to establish a "Composition Curriculum Task Force" composed of supervisors, teachers, and parents. These choices will be influenced by such factors as the size of the school, the nature of your instructional leadership team, and your own time and interest in the project. The only important matter is to be sure that the teachers are aware of your strong commitment and support for the project.

The specific procedures used in strengthening or developing the composition curriculum will depend on the present state of the writing program. I would, however, like to describe a general process found successful in several school districts. I suggest that you and the project team review the process described below, modify it as you see fit, and use it in a way that will best accomplish your own purposes.

Begin by helping English teachers assess the relative importance of writing and the time they wish to allocate to the teaching of writing. The English curriculum embraces so many diverse aspects of communication that some systematic prioritizing seems essential. This need to prioritize is supported by recent research which indicates quite clearly that the time allocated to an area of learning is a critical factor in student achievement. The authors of the research summary *Time To Learn* (Fisher; Berliner; et al., 1980) put it this way: "Other things being equal, the more time allocated to a content area, the higher the academic achievement" (p. 16).

Figure 4.1
Determining Priorities in the English Curriculum

Directions: Listed below are the content areas usually included in the study of English. Indicate by a percentage figure the approximate amount of time you typically devote to instruction in the areas listed. The separate listing does not necessarily imply that you are expected to teach these areas as separate units. Also you need not be exact.

Area	Percentage of time
1. Literature: types of literature, literary terms, history of literature, analysis of literature	_____
2. Grammar: parts of speech, parts of the sentence, types of phrases and clauses, sentence patterns	_____
3. Mechanics: spelling, punctuation, usage	_____
4. Composition: sentence combining, paragraph writing, expository and persuasive essays, other types of writing	_____
5. Language and communication: history of language, communication theory, dialect study, nonverbal communication	_____
6. Speaking: formal and informal speeches, interviewing, panel discussions, debate	_____
7. Listening: listening comprehension, appreciative listening, critical listening	_____
8. Mass media: television, newspapers, radio, magazines	_____
9. Reading: reading comprehension, critical reading, consumer and career reading skills	_____
10. Vocabulary development: learning new words, prefixes and roots, taking vocabulary tests	_____
11. Library use, reference materials: library use, reference books, using the dictionary, retrieving information	_____
12. Other _____	

There are two processes you can use to help teachers think about curricular priorities. One method is to distribute a form like the one shown in Figure 4.1, ask teachers to complete it individually, and then meet to discuss their responses. If you use the form, be sure to stress that it does not attempt to specify how those content areas will be taught, it will not be used for purposes of evaluation, and it does not require exact answers. The other approach is to raise the same issues, without the form, in a department meeting. Have the teachers identify the areas of the English curriculum, ask them to discuss their own curricular priorities, and raise the issue of time allocations.

In either case, the goal is to help teachers reflect about their priorities and their allocation of instructional time. There is, of course, no single correct answer; nor is there a need for schoolwide uniformity. The teachers' answers will be affected by such factors as the nature of the students they teach, the areas emphasized by external examinations, and the teachers' values. For average and above-average students, I believe that teachers should devote between 20 and 35 percent of instructional time to the teaching of writing—but that is simply an opinion that reflects my own conviction that writing is vitally important.

After teachers have made a decision about the total time devoted to the teaching of writing, they should think about how to achieve an optimal balance between and synthesis of what I call an "organic" and a "mastery" approach to the teaching of writing. These terms describe two contrasting approaches to the teaching of writing.

Organic composition program: An approach which emphasizes process and has less concern for product. The student writes in a "writer's workshop," writing chiefly about personal topics, concerned mainly with expressing personal feelings and perceptions. The writing skills are not specified in advance or organized in a predetermined sequence; they are taught as the need arises. The student's writing is usually not graded by the teacher, but is usually shared with peers.

Mastery composition program: An approach which places more emphasis on the product, while giving due attention to the process. The program is carefully structured into writing units that follow a systematic sequence. Writing skills are identified in advance and are taught in relation to a specified assignment. More emphasis is placed on expository and persuasive writing, less on personal writing. The student's writing is graded by the teacher, with specific attention given to the mastery of writing objectives.

Each approach has its enthusiastic supporters, with little empirical research to demonstrate the superiority of one or the other. However, some excellent studies on the general effects of curricula can guide us here. After carefully reviewing the research on so-called innovative curricula, Walker and Schaffarzick reached this conclusion:

> ...different curricula produce different patterns of achievement, not necessarily greater overall achievement. What these studies show, apparently, is *not* that the new curricula are uniformly superior to the old ones, though this may be true, but rather that *different curricula are associated with different patterns of achievement.* Furthermore, these different patterns of achievement seem generally to follow patterns apparent in the curricula.*

Their conclusion suggests that the organic approach would help students become more aware of the process of composing and achieve better results with personal writing, and the mastery approach would make them more concerned with product and achieve greater success in writing expository and persuasive prose. That research and my own

31

*D. F. Walker and J. Shaffarzick, "Comparing Curricula," *Review of Educational Resources,* no. 44 (1974), p. 97.

Figure 4.2

Determining the Balance Between the Organic and Mastery Composition Curricula

Directions: In the diagram below, show what percentage of the composition program should be devoted from grade to grade to the mastery approach. You are to assume that you are making recommendations for the general population. There is no "right" answer. Your answer will depend upon your teaching style, your view of composing, and your teaching experience.

Grade 1	2	3	4	5	6	7	8	9	10	11	12

```
P   100
e    90
r    80
c    70
e    60
n
t    50

M    40
a    30
s    20
t
e    10
r
y     0
```

Figure 4.3
Tonawanda Middle School's Composition Program

I. Common writing activities each semester
   A. Poetry
   B. Journal or other free writings
   C. Creating language activities leading to writing

II. Writing emphasis each semester
   A. Dramatic—Grade 7, Semester 1
      1. Dialogs
      2. Interior monologs
      3. Dramatic monologs
      4. Short scenes
      5. Radio plays, to be audio-recorded
      6. One-act plays, to be rehearsed and enacted

   B. Narrative—Grade 7, Semester 2
      1. Personal experience
      2. Autobiography
      3. Chronicle
      4. Biography
      5. Memoir

   C. Fictional—Grade 8, Semester 3
      1. Recycle of Semesters 1 and 2
      2. Short fiction

   D. Observational-Explanatory—Grade 8, Semester 4
      1. Interviews
      2. Idea writing
      3. Writing about fiction

*Charles R. Cooper, "Tonawanda Middle School's New Writing Program," *English Journal,* November 1976, pp. 56-61.

experience suggest to me that the best composition program will combine both organic and mastery elements in some optimal balance. What is that optimal balance? The answer depends on the students' maturity, ability, and career goals. I believe that the program for younger adolescents should be primarily organic, and the program for mature high school students substantially mastery in emphasis.

It is more important, however, for you and the teacher to consider this issue together. In such discussions you might find the form in Figure 4.2 useful.

If at least part of the composition curriculum will be devoted to a mastery approach, then the next step is to choose the curriculum structure that you think will give the best results. You and your teachers have six models to choose from: discourse-centered; cognitive-based; skill focused; individualized; developmental; and generic. I would like to describe each of these models briefly and then suggest how the strengths of several of them might be combined.

33

Figure 4.4
A Curriculum Sequence Based upon Cognitive Processes

Grade Seven
1. Segmentation and focus: specification and detailing
2. Comparison and contrast: distinctions, incongruities, likenesses

Grade Eight
3. Classification: similarities, labeling
4. Changes: growth, development, metamorphosis

Grade Nine
5. Physical context: nature, effect on feelings
6. Sequence: chronological and logical sequences

Grade Ten
7. Structure analysis—parts, wholes, and their connections
8. Operation analysis—stages, operations, phases

DISCOURSE CENTERED.

I use this term to describe writing curricula based upon or derived from James Moffett's theories of language as explicated in *Teaching the Universe of Discourse* (1968). As Moffett sees communication, it develops hierarchically: from the concrete to the abstract; from the personal to the impersonal; from the past, to the present, to the future; from drama, to fiction, to essays. While he himself rejected the notion of sequential curricula, some curriculum workers have used his theory as a way of conceptualizing and sequencing the curriculum. One of the best attempts to use the Moffett paradigm is the composition curriculm developed for their middle schools by Charles Cooper (1976) and a group of teachers from the Tonawanda (N.Y.) school district. (See Figure 4.3.) A curriculum like Tonawanda's could readily be extended into the high school by emphasizing exposition and argumentation, as the Moffett paradigm would suggest.

COGNITIVE BASED.

34

This model uses a hierarchy of intellectual operations as its framework. Here the structure is perceived not in terms of the nature of discourse but instead as a series of intellectual processes arranged in order of increasing complexity. Such a sequence has been recommended by James M. McCrimmon (1966), who cites Jerome Bruner and Albert Upton as his major theoretical sources. McCrimmon's article suggests how a junior high school composition curriculum could be developed around these cognitive processes; I have drawn upon the work of Lee Odell (1977) and Albert Upton (1978) to add to the high school components. Figure 4.4 outlines the combined sequence.

SKILL FOCUSED.

A skill-focused composition curriculum is one that is designed around a set of discrete writing skills. Specific skills (like "using a topic sentence in an expository paragraph") are identified and then arranged in a sequence of increasing complexity. One of the best skill-focused curricula is that developed by the Chelmsford (Mass.) schools. The Chelmsford "Flow Chart for Compositional Writing" (Chelmsford School District, 1978) identifies 37 specific writing skills, indicates where those skills are introduced and reinforced, and suggests the forms of writing that should be taught.

INDIVIDUALIZED.

The term individualized used here identifies composition curricula built upon a diagnostic-prescriptive model. Most diagnostic-prescriptive models are individualized variants of skill-focused curricula. The curriculum specialist develops a list of specific writing skills, often stated as learning objectives (such as "varies sentence beginnings"), and writes instructional materials for each skill. The teacher compares the first writing sample to the master list of skills, determining which skills are needed by the whole class, which by certain groups, and which by individual students. Based upon this analysis, the teacher determines priority needs and plans a sequence of activities as prescribed by the diagnosis.

The most carefully developed individualized program I have found is the Weehawken (N.J.) "Individualized Language Arts" program (1974) developed by Edwin Ezor. If you and your teachers are interested in an individualized approach, you can consider using the ILA materials or can develop your own. I have developed my own diagnostic grid which could also be used as the basis of an individualized program. (See Figure 4.5.)

DEVELOPMENTAL.

Developmental composition sequences are those based upon a careful analysis of what pupils can and do write. Hailey (1978) points out that too many curriculum sequences are developed by specialists who are "closeted apart from children." He argues for sequences that grow out of holistic assessments of students' writing. As a result of the reports on student writing in the Bay Area Writing Project and his analysis of district curriculum guides, Hailey has been able to identify what he calls "important attributes" and "critical skills" for grades one through eight. Important attributes are the qualities of writing commonly found in the writing of children at a particular grade level; critical skills are those qualities which separate the best papers from the others. Here, for example, is his list for grade seven:

- Important Attributes
  Paragraphs have topic sentences
  Action rises to a climax

Figure 4.5
Diagnostic Grid

Ideas and Content

1. Are the ideas original with the writer? If other sources were used, are the sources properly identified?

2. Does the essay express the sincere convictions of the writer, unless there is an obvious intent to pretend?

3. Are the ideas expressed in an interesting manner so that the reader is motivated to read?

4. Do the ideas and content seem useful for the intended audience?

5. Does the essay respond directly to the assignment given?

Organization

1. Does the essay have a clear and appropriate pattern of organization?

2. Is the organization made clear through effective use of varied transitions?

Sentences

1. Are sentences complete, so that fragments are avoided?

2. Do sentences show correct compounding, with run-ons avoided?

3. Are modifiers placed so that it is clear what they modify?

4. Is pronoun reference clear and specific?

5. Are sentences concise, with wordiness and unnecessary repetition avoided?

6. Are parallel structures used appropriately?

7. Are sentences forceful and direct, with weak passives avoided?

8. Are sentences mature? Are weak compounds and short simple sentences avoided?

Paragraphs

1. Is there an effective introductory paragraph that states or leads into the main idea and begins the essay smoothly?

2. Are all developmental paragraphs fully developed and interesting to read?

3. Are developmental paragraphs coherent, with effective use made of transitions?

4. Do the developmental paragraphs show unity?

5. Is appropriate use made of topic sentences?

6. Is paragraphing used effectively and correctly, so that the reader understands why a new paragraph begins when it does?

7. Is there an effective concluding paragraph that brings the essay to a close?

9. Are sentences varied without being awkward?

10. Are sentences punctuated correctly?

Words

1. Is word choice appropriate to the audience?

2. Is word choice appropriate to purpose?

3. Are words with correct denotation used?

4. Are clear and specific words used, with vague words avoided?

5. Does word choice suggest freshness, with clichés avoided?

6. Do subjects and verbs agree?

7. Do nouns and pronouns agree?

8. Are verb forms correct?

9. Are modifiers correct in form?

10. Are words spelled correctly?

37

Figure 4.6
Composition Curriculum Mapping Form

To the teacher of English language arts: The Composition Task Force wishes to determine what the teachers in this district are teaching in the area of English composition. We have listed below the categories we have decided to use in gathering our data. For each category listed, will you please tell us what writing skills you emphasize in the grade level for which you are responsible. Please list only those major skills which you emphasize for all students. The data will be useful to us in making decisions about the optimal placement of skills and unity.

Teacher's Name _____ Grade_____

Word Choice
_____

Sentence Skills
_____

Paragraphing
_____

Personal and Creative Writing
_____

Exposition
_____

Argumentation
_____

Writing About Literature
_____

Academic Writing
_____

Applied Writing
_____

_____

- Critical Skills
    Logical ability
    Use of figurative language
    Subject-verb agreement
    Control of pronouns
    Sentence variety

GENERIC.

Many schools have developed composition curricula around the types or genres of writing—exposition, argumentation, narration, and description. The rationale is that each of these types requires different skills and should therefore be treated separately. An excellent curriculum based on the generic approach, which also emphasizes the composing processes, is that developed by Frederick Tuttle in collaboration with English teachers from the West Irondequoit (N.Y.) school district (Tuttle, 1977).

No research is available to indicate the superiority of any one of those models or structures. Each has its own advantages. The chal-

38

Figure 4.7
Criteria for Evaluating Scope and Sequence of a Secondary Composition Program

1. Does the composition curriculum reflect the best available knowledge about language development, the composing process, and the teaching of writing?

2. Is the scope of the program sufficiently comprehensive, so that all modes of discourse and elements of composition are emphasized?

3. Does the sequence of units from level to level provide for systematic development of important skills without excessive repetition?

4. Is the sequence of units of study sufficiently responsive to the changing interests and needs of adolescents?

5. Do the scope and sequence of the composition program make adequate provision for any "basic competencies" mandated by the state or local district?

6. Does the curriculum respond adequately to the reasonable expectations of local citizens and employers and emphasize for college-bound students the skills required for successful performance in college?

7. Is the scope and sequence plan easy to understand and implement, focusing only on the essential learnings that require systematic planning?

8. Is the grade by grade distribution of skills and concepts balanced in terms of the expectations for a given grade?

9. Does the placement of units at a given grade level reflect a realistic appraisal of what students are able to achieve at that stage of development?

lenge, therefore, is to find a structure which will embody the advantages of several models and will be usable by the classroom teacher. My own solution has been to devise a curricular structure which includes both the elements of composition and the kinds of writing that secondary teachers usually assign. I therefore suggest a scope and sequence chart built upon these strands:

39

- *Word Choice:* choosing correct and effective words
- *Sentence Skills:* writing correct and effective sentences; using sentence combining techniques
- *Paragraphing:* developing effective paragraphs
- *Personal and Creative Writing:* writing stories, poems, plays
- *Exposition:* writing essays of exposition—process analysis, comparison-contrast, causal analysis, etc.
- *Persuasion:* writing essays of opinion and argumentation

Figure 4.8
The Teaching of Writing: Findings Gleaned
from Research

1. The study of grammar is an ineffective way to teach writing and takes time away from reading and writing (Petrosky, 1977).
2. Frequency of writing in and of itself is not associated with improvement of writing (Haynes, 1978).
3. There is a positive relationship between good writing and increased reading experiences (Blount, 1973).
4. Beneficial results accrue from the use of such prewriting procedures as thinking, talking, working in groups, role playing, interviews, debates, and problem solving (Haynes, 1978).
5. "Teachers should give greater emphasis to the guiding of careful development of a limited number of papers, with attention given to direct methods of instruction and to the solving of communication problems before and during the writing process, rather than on the hurried production of a great number of papers (Haynes, 1978, p. 87)."
6. There is some evidence that sentence-combining practice, without instruction in formal grammar, is an aid to syntactic fluency (Haynes, 1978).
7. While there does not seem to be any evidence to support one revision process over another, there is substantial evidence that the revision process itself is critical in improving writing (Bamberg, 1978).
8. The type or intensity of teacher evaluation of composition is not related to the improvement in writing skill (Bamberg, 1978).
9. Written language is closely related to oral language. Teaching should emphasize and exploit the close connection between written and oral language (Lundsteen, 1976).
10. The quality of students' writing is not affected by positive or negative criticism, but positive comments are more effective than negative ones in promoting positive attitudes toward writing (VanDeWeghe, 1978).
11. Peer evaluation and editing are effective in improving writing skills (VanDeWeghe, 1978).

- *Writing About Literature:* analyzing literary works, writing book reviews and book reports
- *Academic Writing:* writing essay answers, term papers, school reports
- *Applied Writing:* writing letters, memos, résumés, applications.

As I will note later, those elements and types of writing will be used as the basis of composition units which will include specific writing and thinking skills.

Once the choice of curriculum structure has been made, you and the teachers can work together to map the existing curriculum. Fenwick English (1978) defines curriculum mapping as a process of determining what teachers are actually teaching. Although he recommends using the mapping process to monitor and control the curriculum, I believe it should be used as the critical step in building the curriculum. Rather than having a committee of teachers closet themselves in the summer to produce a curriculum guide which will probably not be used, I think we should develop the curriculum from what teachers are actually teaching, building the curriculum from the ground up.

I have found that a form like the one shown in Figure 4.6 is effective in mapping the composition curriculum. Notice that it uses the structures recommended above; it would be modified, of course, if you and the teachers had opted for some other structure.

The results from the mapping project should be collated and displayed on a large wall chart so that you can see what teachers are teaching from grade to grade in the area of composition. The chart will also enable you to detect any serious problems of repetition or omission which need to be rectified before the chart takes final form.

In addition to checking for repetitions and omissions, it is also essential for a committee of teachers and instructional leaders to review the mapping data to be sure that the scope and sequence reflect our best current knowledge about language development and writing ability. I list in Figure 4.7 the criteria which I use in evaluating composition curricula. The revised scope and sequence chart can then be distributed to the teachers for their further review and consideration.

The processes described above should yield a scope and sequence that reflects the informed practice of teachers, responds adequately to state guidelines and parent expectations, and is in accord with major research findings in the teaching of writing. But obviously we need more than a scope and sequence chart. We need materials that will help teachers translate that scope and sequence chart into effective plans for learning. Here I recommend that we not use the standard curriculum guide format. Instead, teachers should cooperate in developing a loose-leaf composition notebook which contains these essential components:

- A copy of the scope and sequence chart.
- A summary of major research findings in the field, like that shown in Figure 4.8.
- The objectives for each unit listed on the scope and sequence chart for that particular grade level.
- Suggestions for responding to and evaluating student writing.

41

Let me explain in more detail the unit objectives referred to above. For each unit in word choice, sentence structure, and paragraphing, teams should specify the important learning objectives. Suppose, for example, that the revised scope and sequence chart indicated in the

Figure 4.9
Unit Objectives, Grade 10: Avoiding Sexist Language

The unit will be structured and taught so as to enable the student to develop the following knowledge and skills:
1. Define "sexist language."
2. Know that language reflects cultural norms and personal biases.
3. Know that sexist language is offensive to women and perpetuates stereotyping.
4. Use career terms that avoid sexual stereotyping (for example, *salesperson,* not *salesman).*
5. Avoid the use of the masculine pronoun when the antecedent could be either feminine or masculine.
   (For example, write: Doctors should consider their patients' feelings, not, The doctor should consider his patients' feelings.)
6. Avoid terms that are patronizing of or condescending to women.

"word choice" strand that there would be a unit of study on "sexist language" in grade 10. The teaching team might then develop a list of objectives like that shown in Figure 4.9.

For the strands based on the kinds of writing, the objectives should be listed in an "assignment sheet" which can be given to students. The assignment sheet specifies the topic and the audience, tells the student which objectives are important, and specifies the grading standards. Figure 4.10 shows a sample assignment sheet for a persuasive essay. These assignment sheets accomplish a two-fold purpose: They remind the teacher which objectives should be emphasized in teaching the unit; and they clarify for the student the qualities expected in a good essay of that type.

Distribute the notebook to the teachers and encourage them to make it their own, adding articles from journals, classroom exercises they have developed, and materials their colleagues have shared with them. The loose-leaf format makes it easy for the notebook to be expanded and revised.

42

The process described above will produce a composition curriculum for the standard required English program. But it can also be used as the basis for elective programs. If graded electives are offered, then the composition units assigned to a particular grade level can be made a part of each elective offered at that level. If nongraded electives are offered, teachers will have to develop record-keeping and diagnostic systems to help them determine which composition units should be taught in a given elective course. Those composition units can also be used in interdisciplinary courses. For example, an interdisciplinary American studies course offered at grade 11 would incorporate the eleventh grade composition units as well as providing for other writing specifically required by the course.

Figure 4.10
Persuasive Essay Assignment

The Assignment: Choose a current issue that interests you and about which you have formed an opinion. Investigate that issue to gather more information and to crystallize your thinking. Identify an audience you wish to persuade and write a persuasive essay or article that advances your arguments and refutes or rebuts the arguments of those likely to oppose your position.

Mastery Objectives: Your persuasive essay should demonstrate that you know how to achieve the following writing objectives:

1. Develop a coherent plan for the essay, arranging your arguments and your rebuttal in a manner that will be most persuasive.

2. Begin the essay in a way that will interest your audience and make clear your position.

3. Advance logical and convincing arguments supported by evidence designed to persuade your audience.

4. Rebut the arguments and evidence likely to be advanced by those opposing your position.

5. Use a tone of language which will seem acceptable and persuasive to your audience.

Standards: Your essay will be read with the above objectives in mind. In addition, you will be expected to show that you can write an essay reasonably free of major errors. You will be given one of three grades:

A—This paper is an excellent paper. It demonstrates that all the objectives have been met; that the writing has a personal style; and that the paper is free of major errors.

B—This paper is a good paper. It demonstrates that the most important writing objectives have been met; that the style is clear; and that there are not more than four major errors.

I—This paper is considered incomplete. It does not demonstrate the mastery of the writing objectives and/or contains more than four major errors. Do the necessary corrective activities and resubmit a revised paper.

Major Errors: For purposes of this assignment, a major error is one of the following, indicated by the symbol noted:

S—A word is misspelled.

FR—A fragment or piece of sentence has been written as a sentence.

R—Two sentences have been run together with incorrect punctuation.

US—A basic error in usage has been made.

π—An error in paragraphing has been made, or a paragraph has not been fully developed.

43

Any of these options make sense as long as we ensure that every student has systematic instruction in composition during each year of secondary school. Since the ability to write develops slowly and seems to require consistent nurturing, I would dissuade schools from trying to teach composition in a one-semester course. Such intensive courses do not ensure long-term development of skills.

44

5. Improving Writing Across the Curriculum

A CONSENSUS EXISTS among the experts that student writing will improve most of all when there is a general emphasis on writing across the curriculum. Instead of pigeonholing writing as something that is done in English class, the most forward-looking schools are developing and implementing cooperating processes whereby writing is an important part of learning in all the disciplines. I therefore would like to describe a process for making writing an important part of learning in all the areas of the school curriculum.

At the outset, however, it might be useful to develop a rationale for such an emphasis: A schoolwide emphasis seems desirable for three reasons. First, if teachers in such disciplines as science and social studies emphasize writing in their classrooms students should improve their understanding of those disciplines, for writing is a way of knowing. The process of writing requires students to systematize what they know, and the act of writing facilitates the discovery of new insights. Writing is an active process and most educators agree that such active processes improve learning.

Second, the student's ability to write will be increased if the student has an opportunity for guided practice in several classrooms, not just in English class. If the art teacher shows the student how to write an evaluation of a painting and the home economics teacher explains how to write an evaluation of a family diet, the student's ability to write evaluative prose will be markedly enhanced. Such an all-school emphasis on writing should also have subtle influences on the students' attitudes toward writing. Too often students believe that good writing is important only in English class and that careless writing is acceptable in other classrooms. An all-school emphasis should go a long way toward eliminating this perception.

Finally, an all-school emphasis on writing, if it is developed and implemented sensibly and effectively, should be a good vehicle for increasing interdepartmental cooperation. Interdepartmental meetings in which teachers discuss the inquiry processes of their disciplines and the kinds of writing important in their fields will help teachers understand their colleagues' work and value their efforts to improve student learning.

Figure 5.1

Schoolwide Assessment of Faculty Practices and Perceptions

1. Listed below are several objectives that might concern the Task Force on a Schoolwide Emphasis on Writing. Next to each objective indicate what priority you think it should have by writing one of these letters:

   H—this should be a *high* priority objective for the task force
   M—this should be a *middle* priority objective for the task force
   L—this should be a *low* priority objective for the task force

   - Help interested teachers in all disciplines learn how to use writing to increase learning in their subject. ___
   - Help English teachers develop and implement plans to improve basic skills in academic writing. ___
   - Help interested teachers learn how to respond to and evaluate writing in their disciplines. ___
   - Develop procedures for scheduling major writing assignments (such as term papers) so that excessive demands are not made upon students. ___
   - Develop a uniform style manual to guide the preparation of major papers in all classrooms. ___

2. Listed below are several writing activities that can be used in several of the disciplines to improve learning in that discipline. For each activity, indicate in the *should use* column the extent to which you think this activity should be used in your subject; then in the *do use* column note the extent to which you do use this activity in your subject. This information, of course, will be used only to assess general faculty perceptions and practices, not to evaluate individual faculty members.

Writing Activities	Should Use				Do Use		
	Great	Moderate	Limited		Great	Moderate	Limited
• Students write during class to clarify, articulate, and confirm their own learning.	___	___	___		___	___	___
• Students write journal entries, letters, reaction sheets as ways of giving feedback to their teachers about their learning.	___	___	___		___	___	___
• Students complete writing exercises that help them learn the inquiry skills important in that discipline.	___	___	___		___	___	___
• Students write class notes based on teacher presentations and class discussions in order to record important information and concepts.	___	___	___		___	___	___
• Students write essay answers in examinations to demonstrate their knowledge.	___	___	___		___	___	___
• Students write longer reports based upon their own investigations as a way of extending their knowledge in that discipline.	___	___	___		___	___	___
• Students write essays and reports that integrate concepts and information from several disciplines.	___	___	___		___	___	___

47

If you are convinced that these reasons are persuasive, then how should you develop and implement such a program? I think the first step is to orient the entire faculty to the general purposes of the program. It is important at the very beginning to understand the following:

- People will not discuss who is to blame for student writing problems. It is assumed that all teachers are doing what they reasonably can to improve student writing.
- No one will develop common grading standards for student writing in the several disciplines. The new emphasis on writing will not in any way restrict the teacher's professional autonomy in matters of student evaluation.
- No department will be compelled to participate in the programs developed. All departments will decide on their own about the level and extent of their participation.
- The program will begin with a general assessment of teacher attitudes and practices; the particular thrust and emphasis of the program will reflect teachers' concerns and wishes.

Once that groundwork has been laid, then you should probably form an interdisciplinary task force to be responsible for general planning, implementation, and evaluation. The task force should be a small working group of perhaps five to seven volunteers representing several of the subject areas. The leader of the task force should be someone who has strong leadership skills, who knows how to conduct effective meetings, and who is strongly committed to the all-school emphasis on writing. It is not essential that the leader be the English department head. In fact, there is some merit in appointing someone who is not an English teacher, so that the project is not perceived as an "English department project."

As suggested above, the first job of the task force should be to make a systematic assessment of faculty practices and perceptions, so that whatever program is planned will respond to perceived needs. Figure 5.1 shows a survey form that should provide you and the task force with the required data.

After systematizing and analyzing the results of that survey, the task force should consult with you and district administrators to determine what resources are available, what constraints exist, and what administrative objectives should be addressed. You should also discuss candidly with the task force how much choice you wish to give faculty members about the level of their participation in accomplishing the objectives. Here you have essentially three options:

- All teachers will be required to participate in the program related to a particular objective.
- Each department will discuss the extent of its participation, and members of that department will be bound by the departmental decision.
- Teachers will decide individually if they wish to participate.

48

Your decision will, of course, be influenced by district policy, your own administrative style, and the nature of the objective.

The task force should then develop a comprehensive report for the entire faculty, indicating what objectives will be addressed, what methods will be used in meeting those objectives, and what options teachers have about their participation. The rest of this chapter explains how the five objectives listed in the survey might be achieved, addressing them in the order in which they are presented in the survey instrument.

1. *Help interested teachers in all disciplines learn how to use writing to increase learning in their classrooms.*

This objective can best be achieved by conducting a series of workshops in which interested teachers share ideas and exchange information about the teaching of writing in their discipline. These workshops should, of course, be organized and conducted so that they meet the criteria identified in Chapter 3, to the extent that the available resources make such workshops feasible.

One of the basic objectives of these interdisciplinary workshops should be to help each participant determine what kind of writing activity will be most productive in his or her classroom, rather than to require a given type of activity for all teachers. It might be useful at this juncture, therefore, to explain in greater detail the seven "writing-across-the-curriculum" activities listed in Figure 5.1.

First, the teacher can use what Weiss and his colleagues (1980) call "learning-centered writing." In learning-centered writing students clarify, articulate, and confirm their own learning by stating in writing the concepts they have learned. Suppose, for example, students discuss in a political science class the way lobbyists operate. The teacher might say to the class: "Some experts have called the lobbyists 'an invisible legislature.' Write in your notebooks a few sentences explaining in what ways lobbyists are an invisible legislature." Note that this kind of writing is quite different from taking class notes; rather than simply recording what the teacher presents, the student writes in order to clarify and articulate what he or she has learned.

Such writing can be brief, perhaps only a few sentences or a short paragraph. It can be done during class at appropriate transition points, or at the end of class as a summarizing activity, or at home as a check on learning. It probably is useful for students to share such writing with each other and for the teacher to use the written statements as part of the classroom transaction.

Second, students can write journal entries, letters, or reaction sheets as ways of giving feedback to their teachers about their learning. Journals have long been used in English classes as means of encouraging students to record their personal observations, feelings, and ideas. Fulwiler (1978) points out that they can be used in all subjects as intellectual diaries in which the students record their questions about what has been taught, their feelings and values as they relate to the

49

concepts, and their ideas about applying what has been learned. In this sense the journal becomes a kind of intellectual diary.

Wotring (1980) had mixed success using the journal to stimulate thinking about high school chemistry; she notes that students do not take readily to journal writing and need a great deal of help in using and learning from the journal-keeping process. Other teachers have found it useful to ask students to write brief letters or complete reaction sheets as ways of eliciting feedback about learning.

The third kind of activity involves the use of carefully structured writing exercises as a means of learning and applying the inquiry skills important in a given discipline. For example, a science teacher might decide that an important inquiry skill in science is the ability to observe accurately and to report those observations in objective language.

The teacher would therefore develop an exercise in which students would first observe and describe objectively a staged classroom encounter and then observe and describe objectively the results of a laboratory experiment. Giroux (1979) has developed some interesting exercises that use writing as a way of understanding and acquiring cognitive skills important in the social sciences. One exercise, for example, helps students understand and write about the concept of "frame of reference" as an important aspect of historiography.

The fourth activity, writing class notes, is widely used in most disciplines; in fact, many educators believe it is overused. The concern here, therefore, is to help teachers understand when notetaking is appropriate and how to improve students' notetaking skills. Teachers who wish to improve these skills should give specific attention to the following techniques and strategies:

- Knowing when to take notes and when not to take notes
- Identifying the teacher's general lecturing and organizing style
- Getting the big picture: using overviews and advance organizers to identify the general plan
- Identifying main ideas and key concepts
- Identifying digressions and irrelevancies
- Identifying important facts and significant details
- Identifying and using examples
- Using a variety of forms for recording notes—idea maps, outlines, diagrams, notecards
- Learning from notes

The fifth method, writing essay answers, is one widely used in English and social studies classes but seemingly in few other subjects. Teachers probably need help in framing essay questions, in grading essay answers, and in teaching students how to write essay answers.

The sixth method, writing longer reports and term papers, is also much abused. Teachers too often assign such papers without teaching students the skills they need to perform successfully. As a result, students waste a great deal of time producing long, thinly disguised summaries of encyclopedia articles. In fact, many educators have recommended that the term paper be abolished for all except the most gifted high school students.

I differ. I believe that all students can learn a great deal about retrieving, evaluating, and synthesizing information as they write library or term papers. However, such learning can best be accomplished only when the teacher observes some sensible policies and practices: identify topics that do not tax student ability and library resources; teach the specific skills needed to write the kind of paper expected; closely monitor student work to reduce the incidence of plagiarism; cooperate with colleagues in other departments in scheduling longer papers so that students are not required to write more than one major paper at a given time. (Some procedures for accomplishing this last objective are explained below.)

Finally, some teachers will wish to use a writing activity that requires students to integrate concepts and information from several disciplines. There are essentially two ways of using such an activity.

First, many schools offer interdisciplinary team-taught courses where such writing activities are a normal part of the learning process. For example, students in an "American Studies" course might be asked to write a paper about the view of everyday life in the colonies presented by diarists of the period.

The other approach is to encourage cooperative projects between teachers of related disciplines. For example, English and science teachers could develop a project in which all sophomores would be expected to write an essay dealing with the ethical aspects of some recent scientific or technological advance.

The usefulness of these activities and approaches will vary with the discipline and the way it is taught. For this reason it seems desirable to give the various departments a choice as to which activities and approaches they will emphasize.

2. *Help English teachers develop and implement plans to improve basic skills in academic writing.*

While each discipline has its own particular set of inquiry skills and its own norms about writing, certain writing skills are basic to all academic writing. These basic academic writing skills, I believe, should be taught in the English classroom in a systematic approach and then applied particularly in each relevant discipline.

Some careful curriculum planning is needed to achieve this objective. One way to begin is to survey all the departments to determine which academic writing skills are required at each grade level. A form like the one shown in Figure 5.2 can be used in making such an assessment. The English department can then use the results in determining the sequence in which the skills will be taught. (Figure 5.3 illustrates one possible sequence that reflects increasing developmental complexity.) Those decisions by the English department can be shared with the rest of the faculty, who can plan their work accordingly, knowing which basic skills have been taught and which have not.

Figure 5.2
Survey of Academic Writing Skills

Directions: Listed below are the writing skills often required in academic writing. Circle those skills that you expect your students to use in writing reports and essay answers.

1. Identify and explain the causes of some phenomenon or major event.
2. Identify and explain the effects of some phenomenon or major event.
3. Compare and contrast two people or concepts.
4. Report on one's own investigations, such as a laboratory experiment or interview.
5. Summarize and synthesize secondary sources in a library or term paper.
6. Explain a concept or abstract idea, using techniques of definition.
7. Explain a process.
8. Summarize an article or a book.
9. Develop a proposal for an investigation.
10. Interpret a symbol, a cartoon, or other nonliteral element.
11. State and explicate a generalization and support it with relevant data.
12. Evaluate one or more objects, using objective criteria.
13. Identify and explain a system of classification, or develop one's own classifications.
14. Demonstrate how a particular generalization applies to one or more specific cases.
15. State and defend an hypothesis to account for some series of events or developments.
16. Explain events in daily life in terms of a principle or theory of the social or natural sciences.
17. Analyze and explain a work of art, an institution, or organization.
18. Summarize and draw generalizations from statistical information presented in charts or tables.
19. Evaluate several different sources of information for objectivity and reliability.
20. State and defend one's position on some controversy relating to a particular discipline.

3. *Help interested teachers learn how to respond to and evaluate writing in their disciplines.*

The issue of responding to and evaluating student writing requires special attention since it often divides faculty members and delays progress toward the more important goal of implementing a schoolwide writing improvement program. One of the best ways of dealing with this issue is for the task force to develop a set of guidelines for schoolwide review and use and then encourage each department to use those guidelines in conducting its own workshops.

The guidelines should be brief, making only these essential points:

- Each teacher should be able to grade written work according to that teacher's standards and expectations for that class and that student. There will be no attempt to mandate a uniform grading system for all written work.
- Teachers should keep in mind the research findings about responding to and grading student writing: the intensity and type of evaluation do not seem to make a difference in improving student writing; peer feedback is just as useful—if not more useful—than teacher feedback; positive feedback is just as effective as negative feedback, and results in more positive attitudes toward writing.
- Since revision is effective in improving writing, teachers in all subjects should require students to revise papers when necessary.
- Students should always be certain that their facts are correct, that their reasoning is sound, that their writing is clear, and that their style is appropriate for academic prose. All teachers should hold students accountable, especially for correctness of information, soundness of reasoning, and clarity of writing. The teacher's expectations concerning stylistic "correctness" will vary from subject to subject and class to class.

The intent of the guidelines, obviously, is to help teachers focus on the most important essentials and to reach agreement about those critical matters. Individual teachers then are free to be as strict or as liberal as they wish about their requirements for correct punctuation, formal usage, and correct spelling.

Once reviewed, modified, and adopted, these guidelines can be used in departmental meetings devoted to the issue of responding and grading. Such meetings will be most productive if the department head duplicates copies of student written work in that discipline, asks teachers to respond to and grade those papers, and then leads the teachers in a discussion of the papers and their reactions to them.

4. *Develop procedures for scheduling major writing assignments (such as term papers) so that excessive demands are not made upon students.*

Students and their parents justifiably complain when two or more major term papers are assigned during the same period of time. The preparation of term papers requires so much time that the students either compromise on matters of quality or let other school work suffer. This vexing problem has some simple solutions. The first step is to persuade teachers to agree on some reasonable policy like the following:

Students should not be expected to prepare and submit two or more long term papers during a given three-week period.

If teachers can agree on such a policy, then implementing it requires only common sense and cooperation. A teacher about to plan for a marking period can simply inquire if students have been informed by

53

Figure 5.3

Recommended Sequence for Academic Writing Skills

7	8	9	10	11	12
Explain process	Develop proposal to investigate	Explain causes	Classify	Interpret symbol, etc.	Define concept
Evaluate object	Report on investigation	Explain effects	State, support generalization	Compare, contrast	State, defend hypothesis
Evaluate sources	Summarize book article	Summarize, generalize from data in tables	Apply generalization to specific cases	State, defend position on controversy	Explain events in terms of theory
			Summarize, synthesize several sources	Analyze work of art, etc.	

other teachers about term papers to be prepared and submitted during that grading period. The teacher can then check with any colleagues involved to adjust schedules and due dates. In schools having interdisciplinary teams it is even a simpler matter to discuss term paper plans and schedules.

If yours is a larger school with relatively little interdepartmental collaboration, then you may wish to formalize these matters. You could require all teachers assigning term papers to complete a form indicating the class and the due date for the paper. These forms would be submitted directly to an administrator familiar with the school's master schedule. This administrator could easily determine if potential conflicts existed and notify the teachers involved, allowing them to work out the conflict or develop cooperative plans for the papers.

5. *Develop a uniform style manual to guide the preparation of major papers in all classrooms.*

This is a relatively minor matter, but it is one that seems to concern teachers. The goal, consequently, should be to deal with the matter as expeditiously as possible. The style manual need not concern itself with matters of punctuation and usage that are dealt with in every English text; rather, it should focus on those matters where there is not a clear consensus about form. First, the task force should agree on a standard heading for all school reports. Second, they should review the several forms available for documenting and citing references. Finally, the task force should agree on the method for listing references or bibliographic material.

The objective here is to simplify matters for teachers and students. If the faculty can agree on uniform styles for headings, citations, and references, then teachers will not have to waste class time teaching their own preferred forms and students will not be expected to master four systems. There are more important matters to teach and to learn.

6. Supervising the Writing Program

ONE OF THE principal's main concerns should be how best to supervise the writing program. Your approach, of course, will be influenced by your own attitudes toward supervision, your perception of your faculty members' strengths, and your other leadership responsibilities.

My own preference is for a supervisory approach that emphasizes collegiality by trusting experienced teachers to monitor their own professional performance. And there is some evidence (e.g., Chung, 1970) that such an approach results in improved teacher morale. I suggest, therefore, an approach that involves three closely related activities; peer monitoring, collegial feedback, and self-appraisal. If you prefer that administrators supervise the program, then you can modify the processes explained below so that you and your assistants play a more active leadership role.

"Peer monitoring" is a process where English teachers work together to share information about student progress from year to year and to report on their own writing programs. Both objectives can be achieved through the use of a cumulative writing folder. If at all possible, the folder should be kept throughout all the secondary grades. However, if it is difficult to secure districtwide cooperation in such a project, you should work at least with your English teachers to develop a cumulative writing folder for your school.

One system that seems to work well uses a manila folder. The school mimeographs a few thousand blank forms like the one shown in Figure 6.1. As these are completed, they are stapled to the folder. The preparation of the folder begins when the student arrives in your school. Under the direction of the English teacher, the student writes his or her name on the tab, staples the first sheet to the folder, and enters the identifying information on the sheet. It then becomes the student's responsibility to keep the folder up-to-date. When the teacher returns a paper, the student enters the appropriate information on the form and puts the composition in the folder.

Some teachers require students to retrieve their own folders from the file when they need them. Other teachers remove the folders when they have papers ready to return, distribute the folders to the class, and then collect and file them when the recording process has been com-

Figure 6.1

Sample Cumulative Writing Record

STUDENT'S NAME *Gwen A. Washington*

Grade *9* Teacher *Barbara Parpart* Class *9-2* School year *1982-83*

Date	Type of Writing	Approx. Length	Topic	Grade	Significant Strength, Weakness
9/15	*Personal narrative*	*350 words*	*First success*	B	*Used dialog well; too many digressions*
10/ 7	*Monolog*	*250 words*	*Morning thoughts*	A	*Used sensory images well; spelling errors*

GRADE 9 SUMMARY: Average grade in English for year: *B*

  Major strength in writing: *Creative use of language; uses vivid images; creates interesting stories*
  Area needing improvement: *Expository and persuasive essays need to be organized more clearly*

Figure 6.2
Observing the Exploring and Planning Stages of the Composing Process

Teacher's Name _____ Class _____

Observer _____ Date of Observation _____

Objective	Teacher's Intent	Observer's Perception	Teacher Activity	Student Behavior Indicating Success	Student Behavior Suggesting Problems
1. Stimulate interest in particular writing assignment.					
2. Help students explore subject, topic, audience, purpose, voice.					
3. Help students retrieve, systematize needed information.					
4. Help students develop and apply both divergent and convergent thinking skills needed in prewriting stage.					
5. Help students decide on content and organization and make appropriate written plans.					
6. Other _____					

59

Figure 6.3

Observing the Teaching of Writing Skills

Teacher's Name _____ Date of Observation _____ Class _____

Observer _____

Objective	Teacher's Intent	Observer's Perception	Teacher Activity	Student Behavior Indicating Success	Student Behavior Suggesting Problems
1. Help students develop and apply divergent and convergent thinking skills needed in drafting stage.					
2. Help students structure, organize, and make coherent the whole composition.					
3. Help students use effective beginning strategies.					
4. Help students develop paragraphs fully and effectively.					

5. Help students make paragraphs coherent and unified. _____ _____ _____ _____ _____

6. Help students use effective concluding strategies. _____ _____ _____ _____ _____

7. Help students write clear, correct, and effective sentences. _____ _____ _____ _____ _____

8. Help students use words appropriate to purpose, audience, and medium. _____ _____ _____ _____ _____

9. Other _____ _____ _____ _____ _____ _____

62

Figure 6.4
Observing the Revising and Sharing Stages of the Composing Process

Teacher's Name _____ Date of Observation _____ Class _____

Observer _____

Objective	Teacher's Intent	Observer's Perception	Teacher Activity	Student Behavior Indicating Success	Student Behavior Suggesting Problems
1. Help students edit each other's work.					
2. Help class understand common writing problems and make appropriate revisions.					
3. Give individual students the assistance they need in making revisions.					
4. Help students share their writing with each other.					
5. Help students prepare manuscripts for final submission and/or publication.					
6. Other _____					

pleted. The goal is to place as much responsibility as possible on the student, with the teacher providing only minimal supervision.

At the end of the year the teacher returns to the student all except the first and last composition written that year. Those two compositions are kept in the folder to provide specific evidence about achievement for the year. The teacher then files all writing folders in the departmental office. When school reconvenes in September and classroom rosters are established, teachers go to the departmental files to secure the composition folders for their students.

The folders help teachers monitor student progress. Teachers should arrange for periodic formative assessment conferences with each student, reviewing the folder and its contents with the student to identify progress and recurring problems.

The folders also help the English department monitor its own writing program. I recommend that the English teachers meet once each quarter to discuss their writing programs, exchange ideas, identify problems, and share representative folders. The folders are also useful in teacher-parent conferences. They can provide parents with specific information about their youngsters' writing achievements.

The second aspect of the peer-directed supervisory process is "collegial feedback." Collegial feedback is a process in which teachers observe and give feedback to each other. Several schools have effectively employed various models of peer supervision, and research indicates that such systems are both feasible and desirable to classroom teachers (Shapiro, 1978).

To facilitate this collegial feedback process, I have developed the three forms shown in Figures 6.2, 6.3, and 6.4. You will notice that the forms are structured around the model of the composing process delineated in Chapter 1, and pay specific attention to teaching writing skills. Although the forms have been developed for collegial feedback they can also be used by a supervisor, department head, or administrator.

The English teacher who wants a writing class observed indicates to the observer which form would be most appropriate for the intended lesson. The teacher then indicates which objectives he or she intends to achieve in the lesson to be observed. A simple check mark next to the appropriate objective and in the column marked "Teacher's Intent" should be sufficient. These matters could be dealt with in a brief pre-observation conference.

The observer would use the appropriate form in visiting the class selected for observation. As the teacher instructs the class, the observer would use a check mark to indicate that he or she had in fact perceived this objective being considered during the class. The observer would also note in the "Teacher Activity" column what the teacher was doing to achieve the objective. Finally, the observer would note in the appropriate columns specific student behaviors suggesting success or problems. The data collected by means of these forms would then be shared with the teacher in a postobservation debriefing.

Figure 6.5
The Teaching of Writing: A Self-Appraisal Instrument

Directions: Listed below are methods and techniques in the teaching of writing that are strongly supported by the research. For each method or technique listed, indicate to what extent it is characteristic of your own teaching. Use this code to record your answers:

xx—I use this method or technique rather consistently and effectively.

x—I use this method or technique often and with moderate effectiveness.

- —I believe I need to use this technique or method more consistently and with greater effectiveness.

Technique or Method	Your Rating
1. I write and share my writing with my students.	_____
2. I have students write in their journals about their personal feelings, experiences, and beliefs.	_____
3. When I give a structured writing assignment I help students explore and plan, and I provide sufficient time for these stages.	_____
4. When I give a structured writing assignment I teach students the skills they need for that particular assignment.	_____
5. When I give a structured writing assignment I encourage students to revise their work, and I provide time for revision.	_____
6. I teach students how to edit each other's work, and I provide time for peer editing.	_____
7. I emphasize the composing process and help students use processes that are effective and productive.	_____
8. I encourage students to share and publish their work, and I provide opportunities for in-class publication.	_____
9. When I evaluate student writing I offer constructive criticism about the important traits, rather than simply calling attention to mechanical errors.	_____
10. I follow departmental guidelines and policies concerning the composition curriculum and the cumulative writing folder.	_____

I believe the strongest aspect of my teaching of writing is _____
_____.

I would like to improve this aspect of my teaching of writing: _____
_____.

The data on the form could be used in the postobservation conference to deal with such issues as the following:

- What objectives did the teacher intend to deal with that were not considered?
- What objectives did the teacher deal with that were not planned in advance?
- To what extent did the activities used relate directly to the perceived objectives?
- What activities seemed most successful?
- What activities seemed least successful?

The observation forms can serve an instructional purpose as well. Since they derive from a model of the composing process and specify important writing skills, they can also be used to help teachers plan for their composing classes. A teacher can feel reasonably sure that if he or she plans and teaches for the objectives listed, students will write better.

The final aspect of the collegial approach is self-appraisal. This process should be a part of, but not a substitute for, the formal summative evaluation conducted by you and your assistants. The process should begin by having English teachers review the criteria listed in Figure 6.5, making whatever modifications they deem appropriate so that the self-appraisal form represents their own best judgment about the essential criteria.

Prior to the evaluation conference teachers would use the criteria to appraise their own teaching of writing, securing whatever objective data they can to support their self-evaluations. For example, teachers may wish to get student feedback about their teaching of writing, using a form like that shown in Figure 2.3. The results of the self-appraisal should be used in the evaluation conference you hold with English teachers at the end of the semester or school year.

These three processes—peer monitoring, collegial feedback, and self-appraisal—should be a major help to you and your staff in monitoring the writing program.

7. Working with Parents To Improve Student Writing

A NY NEW PROGRAM will be more successful if it has the support and understanding of the parents. And parent understanding is especially important for writing programs, since many of the approved practices in teaching and grading student writing are at odds with generally accepted public beliefs about these issues. This chapter will identify five main objectives of a program to achieve parent support and suggest some specific ways by which those objectives might be achieved.

Develop Parent Understanding

The first objective is to develop parent understanding of the program. As noted above, parents typically will have many questions about such matters as grading, the study of grammar, and the frequency of writing. Unless these issues are confronted parents may have strong reservations about the writing program. Probably the best way to achieve this objective is through a parent meeting in which the topics can be discussed openly. You know what kinds of meetings work best with your parents; an agenda similar to the one shown in Figure 7.1 illustrates one kind of program that has worked well in several schools.

A question-and-answer sheet like that shown in Figure 7.2 can also be very useful. It identifies the questions parents ask most often and responds to those questions in terms that parents can understand. Such a question-and-answer sheet can be distributed at parent meetings, included in a parent newsletter, or made part of a special publication on the teaching of writing.

Teachers and other program participants may need some special help in responding to parent questions about marking papers and the study of grammar, since these issues seem to generate strong feelings. The important point here is to listen carefully and accept parent concerns, and to respond professionally without becoming defensive or condescending. This exchange illustrates the tone that is desired:

"I don't care what you people say. I learned to write by diagraming sentences and studying the parts of speech."

"I certainly don't question your experience. Probably some people do learn to write by a carefully guided study of the language. But

Figure 7.1
Agenda for Parent Meeting on the Teaching of Writing

1. Greetings and overview of program	Principal
2. Brief presentations (10 minutes each)	
1. An all-school emphasis on writing	Assistant principal
2. An overview of the composition curriculum	English department head
3. How one teacher teaches writing	English teacher
3. Small-group discussions to share ideas and identify issues (15 minutes)	An English teacher and a parent as co-leaders
4. Responses to small-group questions (15 minutes)	Panel of English teachers and students
5. Informal discussions for those who wish to stay	

the experience of our teachers, working with our students, supports the research that suggests learning grammar doesn't help most students improve their writing. I'll encourage our teachers to keep an open mind about the issue and to continue to explore how their students best learn to write."

It is also important at such meetings to encourage dialog between teachers and parents. Teachers should see that one of the goals of such a session is to identify parent concerns and to solicit parent suggestions. The small-group discussions are a useful means of identifying such concerns. A recorder in each group should be sure to list all questions and suggestions. Those that are not dealt with in the panel response should be answered in a follow-up newsletter.

Build Parent Support

The second objective is to build parent support for the program. When parents understand the program you and your staff need to work actively to mobilize support for what you are doing. Parents who support the writing program will be welcome allies at budget hearings. Programs for building support should include the following:

- Results of holistic assessments,
- Displays of student writing and student publications,
- Brief presentations by experts from outside the school system who support the general thrust of the program,
- Brief demonstrations of writing lessons by classroom teachers,
- Poetry and short story readings by student writers,
- Videotapes of the composing process, followed by discussions of the composing process.

Clearly, the intent of such programs is to build parent support— but to do so in a professional way.

Figure 7.2
Parent Question-and-Answer Sheet

How often will my son or daughter write in school?

Some writing will be done every day, in almost every major subject your son or daughter is studying. At times the writing will be very brief; at other times, more extended.

What kinds of writing will be done in the English class, and how often will my child write compositions?

In most English classes the students will be writing every day. Some of the writing will be related to what they are studying in English. Some of the writing will be informal, as they write briefly about their personal ideas and experiences. About nine to 12 times a year they will be taught a carefully planned composition unit and will be expected to write a longer story or essay as an outcome of that unit.

Will my son or daughter be required to write about personal or family matters?

Teachers often suggest that students write about what they have experienced, what they feel, and what they believe, since such topics are often more appealing to students. However, no student is ever required to write about personal or family matters which he or she may not wish to discuss.

Will all my child's writing be graded?

The writing the students do in relation to the content of their courses will often be corrected in class. The informal writing will usually not be graded, but students will have an opportunity to read their informal writing to each other. The major essays they write will be graded.

Why don't teachers correct all the mistakes on student papers?

Teachers may not correct a student mistake for one of two reasons. First, they may want the student to concentrate on certain other major problems, and a paper filled with too many corrections and suggestions is often confusing. Second, many teachers believe that students learn more when they find and correct their own mistakes.

Will students grade each other's papers?

Students will often work together in a group to share ideas, to read their writing, and to offer suggestions to each other. Sometimes a student "editor" will help a classmate correct mistakes in spelling and punctuation. Occasionally a teacher may suggest to the students that they evaluate the writing with a grade, but the official grade for a paper is always given by the teacher.

69

Why don't teachers teach more grammar as a way of improving writing?

The study of grammar helps students understand how the language functions and assists teachers in communicating with students about their writing. However, the study of grammar does not seem to be an effective way of learning how to write. Our English teachers, therefore, do not overemphasize the study of grammar. It seems more important to help students learn how to read and write more effectively.

Identify Parent Talents

The third objective is to identify and use parent talents in strengthening the writing program. Parents who are interested and competent can be used in a variety of ways. Those who use writing in their careers can discuss with students why writing is important in the business world. Parents who write professionally can meet with interested students to talk about their work and their own composing processes. And parents who write well can assist English teachers as "writers' aides," helping students edit their work, guiding group discussions of writing, and working with individual students who need help.

Such parent volunteer programs need to be carefully planned and well coordinated, since a hastily conceived and poorly executed program can backfire. Such a project should be the cooperative effort of the parents' group and the English department. A small task force can begin by surveying teachers to determine their interests and needs. They can then survey parents (and other citizens) to identify talents and resources. The survey data can be used in matching teacher needs with parent resources.

Develop Parent Understanding

The fourth goal is to help parents understand how they can best help their children improve their writing. Such collaborative efforts have paid off in "parents-as-partners" reading programs, and their obvious benefits could assist the writing program. The suggestions listed in Figure 7.3 could be shared in parent meetings, discussed in "meet-your-child's-teacher" programs, and disseminated in newsletters and flyers. The major concern here is to stress that the school and the home are partners in a very important enterprise, not to place the responsibility on parents' shoulders.

70

Perhaps a clarifying note is needed here about suggestion five in Figure 7.3. The term "edit" here is used to mean "correct mistakes in form." This is a legitimate form of help that parents can give, since all writers need an editor, someone who can take an objective look at the writing. Parents can provide that help, other family members can assist, and classmates can also perform that function. In order to legitimize editing and to stress its useful functions, many teachers require all final drafts to carry the note, "Edited by _____."

Figure 7.3
What Parents Can Do To Improve Student Writing

1. Encourage all members of the family to use writing as one way of keeping in touch: writing letters, memos, notes, and messages.
2. Develop family writing projects: keeping family diaries, writing in family journals, recording family narratives, writing family poems.
3. Read together as a family, encouraging family members to read, and building a family library.
4. Post writing of family members on bulletin board in the home.
5. Edit children's writing when help is requested and encourage children to use family dictionary to check spelling and capitalization.
6. Set up a "writing center" in the home where family members can write undisturbed: a quiet spot, with a good writing surface, a desk chair, and reference books.
7. Encourage children to take time to explore, plan, and revise when they write.
8. Encourage children to read to the family early drafts of their writing and help family members give each other constructive feedback.
9. Discuss books and writers, and emphasize the value of writing.
10. Keep in close touch with the school about children's progress in writing.

Provide Assistance to Parents

Finally, the school should provide assistance to those parents who want to improve their own writing. Such assistance can be provided through regular adult school offerings, through special PTA seminars, or through informal parent-led groups. Three levels of offerings might be considered: basic writing, for those who want to develop basic writing skills; career writing, for those who want to emphasize career-related forms; and creative writing, for those who want to write poetry, short stories, and personal essays.

Through such a multifaceted approach, the schools can clearly convey the message that they care about writing and that they see the parents as partners in this important enterprise of helping students learn to write better.

8. Improving Your Own Writing

YOUR OWN WRITING should be a matter of continuing concern. If you write clearly and effectively you will communicate better, and will serve as a model for all those in the school who are concerned about writing.

Understanding the special features of writing and realizing the implications of those features for communication effectiveness is important. Three features make the written word very special:

- Writing tends to be a one-way process of communication. Speech is interactive; the spoken word flows both ways. The response to a written statement, if it is made at all, is often delayed for several days.
- Writing is permanent. The spoken word vanishes as soon as it is said, unless it is captured on tape. The written word usually lasts; it is there for all to see long after it has been written. You know what you wrote yesterday; it is there in front of you. You forget what you said 10 minutes ago; it is gone forever.
- Writing lacks the nuances of speech. When you speak, you can use pause, tone, inflection, and volume; you add to the spoken word your smile, your frown, your wink. When you write, you have only words and punctuation marks to convey your meaning.

Writing is not superior or inferior to speaking. It is simply different. And those differences suggest quite clearly that there is a time to write and a time not to write. And there are times, of course, when you use both the spoken and the written word to convey the same message. The suggestions in Figure 8.1 are offered as guidelines to help you decide when you should speak, when you should write, and when you should use both forms.

Suppose, for example, that you wish to reprimand a teacher who has been derelict in monitoring student attendance. You sense that this is a time when you want feedback, but you also want a permanent record. So you call in the teacher for a conference, express the concern, listen to the teacher's excuses, and work out together with the teacher a plan for remedial action. Then you make a note in the teacher's personnel file: "Conferred with Jones: discussed problem of carelessness

73

Figure 8.1
Using Written and Spoken Communication

In general, it is probably better to write when . . .

1. You want a permanent record of the communication.
2. You want to convey some important factual information which should be remembered.
3. You are concerned primarily with conveying information, not with getting feedback and reaction.
4. You wish to reach a large audience that cannot easily be reached by face-to-face communication.
5. You want the audience to be able to process the information quickly.
6. You are communicating with an audience that is literate and that values the written word.

In general, it is probably better to speak when . . .

1. You are not concerned with permanency.
2. You wish to persuade or inspire an audience for whom recall of the details is not important.
3. You want feedback, response, and questions.
4. You want to reach a smaller audience.
5. You are not concerned with speed of processing.
6. You are communicating with an audience that is not oriented to print and that places more value on face-to-face communication.

in monitoring attendance. Jones attributed problem to high level of activity at start of class; worked out a solution which he will implement following week.''

Or consider a second example: The superintendent has announced a set of rather detailed procedures for handling parent complaints about instructional materials used in the classrooms. You are expected to inform the faculty. You summarize the procedures in a one-page handout; distribute it at the beginning of a faculty meeting; give the teachers a few minutes to read it; and then take time for questions and discussion. The handout has helped them get the information quickly and will help them remember it; the discussion has given them a chance to clear up misunderstandings. (In such a situation do not, of course, commit the cardinal administrative sin of reading aloud to them what they can read for themselves.)

If you have decided to use the written word as a primary means of communicating you should follow a systematic process for writing the message. Be sure to allow yourself enough time to follow this step-by-step procedure:

1. Assemble all the facts and information you need for the message.
2. Determine the purpose of the message. Do you write to inform, report, persuade, express feelings, explain, get attention?

3. Consider the audience. Weigh such factors as these: maturity, intelligence, interest in the subject or topic, attitude toward you and the school, feelings about the issue, present knowledge about the subject.
4. Consider the context for the message and how it will affect the message and the readers. How will the message be delivered? What other communications will be received at the same time? When will the message be received?
5. After weighing all these factors, develop a plan for what you wish to write. Do not worry about making fancy outlines; simply make some brief notes or draw a sketch. The important thing is to formalize all the decisions you have made into a tentative plan.
6. Write your first draft. As you write continue to rethink your plan. Revise as you write, but revise for content and organization. Don't worry about spelling and punctuation until you have finished.
7. When you have finished the first draft, go back and revise once more. This time check carefully for form as well as content, tone, and organization.
8. Ask a trusted colleague to edit what you have written and to give you feedback. Ask your colleague to be especially sensitive to the tone: Does the message sound the way you want it to sound?
9. Revise the message for the last time, embodying the suggestions and revisions of your colleague-editor. Prepare the message for reproduction and dissemination.
10. After the message has been delivered, try to get some evaluative feedback. Was the content understood? Did the message have its desired impact?

Those general procedures should be useful in most situations. However, you face a special challenge in writing for students, teachers, and parents; and that special challenge perhaps suggests the need for a closer examination of these three communication contexts.

You should write to students and for students. Do not write simply to scold them for misbehavior. It is important for students to see you as someone who writes, who likes to write, and who writes to communicate positive messages. The particular occasion and format you choose will depend on the size of the school and the communication channels available to you. You may wish to write a weekly bulletin that conveys your personal view of how things are going at school. You may find that a monthly newsletter for students is more appropriate.

When I was principal I found that the best way for me to write to students was through a column in the student newspaper called "From the Principal's Desk." It was a potpourri of brief items: conferences I had attended, students I had talked with, books I had read and enjoyed, school problems that concerned me, teachers and students I felt deserved special commendation, short original poems, comments about important national events and local affairs.

75

Figure 8.2
Ten Don'ts for Improving Your Written Communication

1. Don't write memos to the entire faculty complaining about a problem that only a few are causing. Talk directly with the offenders.
2. Don't write a memo to a teacher scolding him or her about some minor problem. Talk to the teacher, identify the problem, listen, work out a solution together.
3. Don't mail letters written in the heat of anger. Write an angry letter, put it aside for a few hours, and then throw it away.
4. Don't try to win the battle of words with representatives of the news media. If they seriously distort the facts, write a brief letter of correction. Remember that they always have the last word.
5. Don't overemphasize noninstructional matters in your written communications. What you write about indicates what you care about; remember that your business is teaching and learning, not operating a factory.
6. Don't send out important letters, announcements, or bulletins that have not been read and reviewed by someone you trust. Remember that even Hemingway needed a good editor.
7. Don't overuse educational jargon with faculty members—and don't use it at all with parents. Jargon helps insiders communicate with each other—but it confuses and annoys the rest of the world.
8. Don't put in writing something you may later wish could be taken back. Remember that the written word endures.
9. Don't clutter teachers' mailboxes and minds with unnecessary communications.
10. Don't substitute memo-writing for problem solving. Remember Glatthorn's law: The number of memos written is in inverse proportion to the number of problems solved.

Your written messages to faculty members in general should be relatively brief and few in number. Teachers justifiably complain about the volume of memos and announcements that clog their mailboxes. Begin to simplify administrative communications by reviewing the faculty handbook. Be sure you have enough detail on such important matters as how to handle classroom discipline problems and how to deal with parent complaints, two areas where teachers seem to prefer detailed policy guidelines.

Include all the specific information teachers need: room numbers, telephone numbers, school closing procedures, crisis management procedures, school calendar, guidelines on teacher absences, and the like. Eliminate material that is better left to staff development sessions. The faculty handbook is not the place to explain how to teach, how to make lesson plans, or how to arrange an attractive bulletin board.

Your memos to the faculty should include only matters of general information important to all teachers. Write such memos and your "principal's bulletin" in a clear, succinct style. Use lists instead of long paragraphs. Number items so that they stand as separate points. Do not use memos to the faculty or your "principal's bulletin" to scold a few teachers, complain about problems, or make surprise announcements. In general all such matters are better handled in face-to-face spoken communication.

Writing to parents poses a special problem because you are writing to such a varied audience. In sending out general communications like newsletters and announcements, strive especially to be clear and direct. Avoid educational jargon. Parents either are confused or annoyed by such terms as *mainstreaming, individualized instruction, humanistic education, classroom management.* Write simply without being patronizing and condescending. Keep your sentences short and your words specific.

The following two examples illustrate the importance of clear communication:

- We would like to inform parents that the educational portion of the next parents' meeting will be devoted to a panel presentation and group discussion of the instructional implications of mainstreaming. An examination of the peer acceptance and peer interaction in mainstreamed educational settings will also be included.
- What happens when children with handicaps are placed in "regular" classrooms? How do the other children react? How does the teacher teach differently? These questions will be examined at the next parents' meeting. There will be a panel presentation by teachers and parents, followed by audience questions and discussion.

The second version is clearly superior. It is more direct; it is phrased in terms that interest and make sense to parents. It is easier to read, but it is not condescending or childish.

One of the most difficult writing problems is writing a letter that contains some unpleasant news to a parent. To begin with, keep in mind the general principle that bad news is better presented in a face-to-face conference. If that is not possible, then a telephone call is the next best choice. If you have to write a "bad news" letter either because a personal contact is not possible or because you want documentation, then take special pains to be sure you present the news with tact and consideration.

Begin the letter by stating very directly the purpose of the letter. Insofar as possible, avoid including too many specific details of misbehavior; give only as much information as you need and save the details for a follow-up conference. Be as objective as possible in your account; avoid labeling and making judgments. Close the letter by indicating what steps you wish to take and expressing a shared concern for the student's success in school. The sample letter shows one way of handling a delicate situation.

Sample Letter

Dear Mr. and Mrs. Walker:

I am writing to inform you about some recent problems at school that have involved your son, John, and to invite your co-operation in helping us work out the problems together. I have tried on three occasions to call you this past week but have not been able to make contact.

As John may have told you, he has been involved in four separate incidents in his English class during the past few weeks. In each case, according to Miss Williams, his English teacher, John seemed to have provoked the conflict with his classmates. None of these incidents by itself was serious enough to require suspension, but we think now it might be very helpful to discuss the problem with you and John.

I would therefore appreciate it very much if you would call me to arrange for a conference. Since both of you work, I would be happy to work out a time that would enable at least one of you to attend.

I know you are concerned, as we are, that John achieve a good record at school, and we want to do all we can to work with you in making that possible.

Finally, you may wish to keep handy the list of "don'ts" shown in Figure 8.2. It includes most of the important points about effective written communication.

References

Abrahamson, R. F. *The Effects of Formal Grammar Instruction vs. the Effects of Sentence-combining Instruction on Student Writing: A Collection of Evaluative Abstracts of Pertinent Research Documents.* Houston: University of Houston, 1977. (ERIC Document Reproduction Service No. ED 145 450.)

Bamberg, B. "Composition Instruction Does Make a Difference: A Comparison of the High School Preparation of College Freshmen in Regular and Remedial English Classes." *Research in the Teaching of English* 12 (1978): 47-59.

Bechtel, J. B. *Videotape Analysis of the Composing Process of Six Male College Freshman Writers.* Des Moines, Iowa: Midwest Regional Conference on English in the Two-Year College, 1979. (ERIC Document Reproduction Service No. ED 177 558.)

Berman, P., and McLaughlin, M. W. "Federal Programs Supporting Educational Change." In *Implementing and Sustaining Innovations.* Washington, D.C.: U.S. Office of Education, R-1589, No. 8, HEW, 1978.

Blount, N. "Research on Teaching Literature, Language, and Composition." In *Second Handbook of Research on Teaching,* edited by R. M. Travers. Chicago: Rand McNally, 1973.

Chelmsford, Mass., Public Schools. *Flow Chart for Compositional Writing.* Chelmsford, Mass.: Chelmsford Curriculum Office, 1978.

Chung, K. S. "Teacher-centered Management Style of Public School Principals and Job Satisfaction of Teachers." Paper presented at meeting of American Educational Research Association, Minneapolis, Minn., 1970.

Cooper, C. R. "Measuring Growth in Writing." *English Journal* 64 (1975): 111-120.

Cooper, C. R. "Tonawanda Middle School's New Writing Program." *English Journal* 65 (1976): 56-61.

Crowley, S. *Components of the Composing Process.* Philadelphia, Pa.: Conference on College Composition and Communication, 1976. (ERIC Document Reproduction Service No. ED 126 514.)

Daly, J. A., and Miller, M. D. "The Empirical Development of an Instrument To Measure Writing Apprehension." *Research in the Teaching of English* 9 (1975): 242-249.

Diederich, P. B. *Measuring Growth in English.* Urbana, Ill.: National Council of Teachers of English, 1974.

Duke, D. L., and Corno, L. "Evaluating Staff Development." In *Staff Development/Organization Development,* edited by B. Dillon-Peterson. Alexandria, Va.: Association for Supervision and Curriculum Development, 1981.

Emig, J., and King, B. *Emig-King Writing Attitude Scale for Students.* New Brunswick, N.J.: Rutgers University, 1979.

English, F. *Quality Control in Curriculum Development.* Arlington, Va.: American Association of School Administrators, 1978.

Fisher, C. W., Berliner, D. C., et al. "Teaching Behaviors, Academic Learning Time, and Student Achievement: An Overview." In *Time To Learn,* edited by C. Denham and A. Lieberman. Washington, D.C.: National Institute of Education, 1980.

Fulwiler, T. "Journal Writing Across the Curriculum." Paper presented at the Conference on College Composition and Communication. Denver, Colo.: March 1978. (ERIC Document Reproduction Service No. ED 161 073.)

Giroux, H. A. "Teaching Content and Thinking Through Writing." *Social Education* 43 (1979): 190-193.

Graves, D. H. "An Examination of the Writing Processes of Seven Year Old Children." *Research in the Teaching of English* 9 (1975): 227-241.

Hailey, J. *Teaching Writing K Through 8.* Berkeley, Calif.: University of California, 1978.

Hall, G. E.; George, A. A.; and Rutherford, W. L. *Measuring Stages of Concern About the Innovation: A Manual for Use of the SOC Questionnaire.* Austin, Texas: Research and Development Center for Teacher Education, University of Texas, 1977.

Haynes, E. F. "Using Research in Preparing To Teach Writing." *English Journal* 67 (1978): 82-88.

Hendrickson, L. "Procedures and Results of an Evaluation of Writing." *Educational Evaluation and Policy Analysis* 2 (1980): 19-29.

Hunt, D. E. "A Conceptual Systems Change Model and Its Application to Education." In *Experience, Structure, and Adaptability,* edited by O. J. Harvey. New York: Springer, 1966.

Individualized Language Arts. Weehawken, N.J.: Weehawken Board of Education, 1974.

Jones, L. L., and Hayes, A. E. "How Valid Are Surveys of Teacher Needs?" *Educational Leadership* 37 (1980): 390-392.

Joyce, B. R., and Showers, B. "Improving Inservice Training: The Messages of Research." *Educational Leadership* 37 (1980): 379-382.

Klopf, G. *Needs of the Adult Learner.* New York: Bank Street College, 1979.

Knowles, M. *The Adult Learner: A Neglected Species.* Houston, Texas: Gulf, 1978.

Koziol, S. M., Jr. *PCRP Assessment Survey.* Harrisburg, Pa.: Pennsylvania Department of Education, 1981.

Lawrence, G. *Patterns of Effective Inservice Education: A State of the Art Summary of Research on Materials and Procedures for Changing Teacher Behaviors in Inservice Education.* Tallahassee, Fla.: Florida Department of Education, 1979.

Lundsteen, S. W., ed. *Help for the Teacher of Written Composition (K-9): New Directions in Research.* Urbana, Ill.: National Council of Teachers of English, 1976.

McCrimmon, J. M. "A Cumulative Sequence in Composition." *English Journal* 55 (1966): 425-434.

Metzger, E. *The Composing Process of Students Grade 7, Grade 10, and College.* New York State English Council, 1976. (ERIC Document Reproduction Service No. ED 132 589.)

Mischel, T. "A Case Study of a Twelfth-grade Writer." *Research in the Teaching of English* 8 (1974): 303-314.

Moffett, J. *Teaching the Universe of Discourse.* Boston: Houghton Mifflin, 1968.

Mullis, I. V. *The Primary Trait System for Scoring Writing Tasks.* Denver, Colo.: National Assessment of Educational Progress, 1974.

Myers, M. *A Procedure for Writing Assessment and Holistic Scoring.* Urbana, Ill.: National Council of Teachers of English, 1980.

Newkirk, T. "Grammar Instruction and Writing: What We Don't Know." *English Journal* 68 (1978): 46-48.

Newlove, B. W., and Hall, G. E. *A Manual for Assessing Open-ended Statements of Concern About an Innovation.* Austin, Texas: Research and Development Center for Teacher Education, University of Texas, 1976.

Odell, L. "Measuring Changes in Intellectual Processes as One Dimension of Growth in Writing." In *Evaluating Writing: Describing, Measuring, and Judging,* edited by L. Odell and C. Cooper. Urbana, Ill.: National Council of Teachers of English, 1977.

Perl, S. "The Composing Processes of Unskilled College Writers." *Research in the Teaching of English* 13 (1979): 317-336.

Petrosky, A. "Measuring Effects of Instruction in Pre-writing." *Research in the Teaching of English* 8 (1974): 228-240.

Petrosky, A. "Grammar Instruction: What We Know." *English Journal* 66 (1977): 86-88.

Pianko, S. "A Description of the Composing Processes of College Freshman Writers." *Research in the Teaching of English* 13 (1979): 5-22.

Santmire, T. E. *Developmental Differences in Adult Learners: Implications for Staff Development.* Lincoln, Nebr.: University of Nebraska, 1979.

Sawkins, M. W. "What Children Say About Their Writing." In *The Writing Processes of Students,* edited by W. T. Petty and P. P. Finn. Amherst, N.Y.: State University of New York at Buffalo, 1975.

Shapiro, J. "A Differentiated Supervision Model." Doctoral dissertation, University of Pennsylvania, 1978.

Sommers, N. "Revision Strategies of Student Writers and Experienced Adult Writers, 1980." *College Composition and Communication* 31 (1980): 378-387.

Stallard, C. K. "An Analysis of the Writing Behavior of Good Student Writers." *Research in the Teaching of English* 8 (1972): 206-218.

Stotsky, S. L. "Sentence Combining as a Curricular Activity: Its Effect on Written Language Development and Reading Comprehension." *Research in the Teaching of English* 9 (1975): 20-71.

Tuttle, F. F., Jr. *Written Composition: Integrated Approach Following the Composing Process, Low/Average Students, Ninth Grade.* West Irondequoit, N.Y.: 1977. (ERIC Document Reproduction Service No. ED 146 587.)

Upton, A. *Creative Analysis.* New York: Dutton, 1978.

Van De Weghe, R. *Research in Written Composition: Fifteen Years of Investigation.* Las Cruces, N.M.: New Mexico State University, 1978.

Walker, D. F., and Schaffarzick, J. "Comparing Curricula." *Review of Educational Resources* 44 (1974): 83-112.

Weiss, R. H., et al. "Writing To Learn." Paper presented at the meeting of the American Educational Research Association, Boston, Mass., April 1980.

Wolter, D. R., and Lamberg, W. J. *Research on the Effect of Feedback on Writing: Review and Implications.* Austin, Texas: University of Texas, 1976.

Wotring, A. M. "Writing To Think About High School Chemistry." Master's thesis, George Mason University, Fairfax, Va., 1980.

82

Resources in the Testing and Teaching of Writing

The following is a selective list of currently available school resources in the testing and teaching of writing. In each case the materials listed have been checked for both quality and availability. The sources are listed alphabetically by school or district name; the title of any publication and the name and address of the office or person to be contacted are identified. In some cases there is a charge for the publication; write to the office identified for current information about prices.

SECONDARY ENGLISH COMPOSITION GUIDES

The following schools or school districts have recently developed secondary composition curriculum guides covering the grade levels indicated in the parentheses.

Allegheny, Pa., Intermediate Unit. (6-12). *Project Write.* Carolyn Piazza, 2 Allegheny Center, Pittsburgh, Pa. 15212.

Chelmsford, Mass. (K-12). *Composition: K-12.* A. James Temmallo, Language Arts Coordinator, Chelmsford Public Schools, 31 Princeton St., North Chelmsford, Mass. 01863.

Darien, Conn. (7-12). *Curriculum Guide, Junior High English.* Coordinator of Language Arts K-12, Darien Public Schools, P.O. Box 1167, Darien, Conn. 06820.

East Brunswick, N.J. (K-12). *Composing Process Curriculum.* Language Arts Supervisor, East Brunswick Public Schools, East Brunswick, N.J. 08816.

Frederick, Md. (7-12). *Using Student Team Learning. Dictation.* J. Richard Lewis, Supervisor Federal Program, Frederick County Schools, Frederick, Md. 21701.

Lincoln, Nebr. (9-12). *The Writer's Gallery.* Project Director, Writer's Gallery, Lincoln Public Schools, 2229 J Street, Lincoln, Nebr. 68510.

Los Angeles, Calif. (7-12). *Compose Yourself: A Plan for Instruction in Written Composition, Grades 7-12.* Roger Hyndman, Instructional Specialist, English, Los Angeles Unified School District, P.O. Box 3307, Terminal Annex, Los Angeles, Calif. 90051.

Madison, Wisc. (Middle School). *A Functional Writing Program for the Middle Grades.* Joanne Yatvin, Crestwood School, Madison, Wisc. 53703.

Neshaminy, Pa. (K-12). *Writing To Be Read: A Curriculum for Teaching the Writing Process.* Supervisor of Language Arts, Neshaminy School District, Langhorne, Pa. 19047.

Newark, N.J. (K-12). *Reading and Writing.* Director, Project READ/WRITE, Hawkins St., Newark, N.J. 07105.

San Antonio, Texas (K-12). *North East Independent School District K-12 Composition Curriculum.* Deurene Morgan, North East Independent School District, 10333 Broadway, San Antonio, Texas 76286.

Pottstown, Pa. (K-12). *Language Arts Guide, K-12.* District Wide Committment and Corresponding Program, Pottstown School District, Pottstown, Pa. 19464.

Walnut Creek, Calif. (9-12). *9-12 Sequence of Instruction, Las Lomas High School.* Jean Jensen, English Department, Chair, Las Lomas High School, Walnut Creek, Calif. 94596.

WRITING ACROSS THE CURRICULUM

The following schools or school districts have developed programs to emphasize writing in several school subjects offered in the grade levels indicated in parentheses.

East Amherst, N.Y. (10-12). *Writing Across the Curriculum.* Amy Doty, Williamsville East High School, 151 Paradise Rd., East Amherst, N.Y. 14051.

Hanover, N.H. (10-12). *Writing Across the Curriculum.* Robert McCarthy, Principal, Hanover High School, Hanover, N.H. 03755.

Hatboro-Horsham, Pa. (7-12). *Writing in the Content Areas.* Gary Ruch, Reading Supervisor, Hatboro-Horsham School District, Horsham, Pa. 19044.

STAFF DEVELOPMENT PROGRAMS IN THE TEACHING OF WRITING

The following schools or school districts have ongoing staff development programs in the teaching of writing.

Andover, Mass. *Improving Writing Skills.* Mary Poulin, The Network, 290 S. Main St., Andover, Mass. 04216.

East Brunswick, N.J. Language Arts Coordinator, East Brunswick Public Schools, East Brunswick, N.J. 08816.

Huntington Beach, Calif. *In-Service Training.* J. Kenneth Jones, Huntington Beach Union High School, 10251 Yorktown Ave., Huntington Beach, Calif. 92646.

ASSESSMENT OF WRITING

The following schools or school systems use holistic or primary trait scoring methods to assess student writing.

Beaverton, Oreg. *Writing Assessment.* Coordinator of Program Evaluation, Beaverton School District, Beaverton, Oreg. 97005.

Bloomington, Minn. *Writing Assessment.* Director of Evaluation, Bloomington Schools, 8900 Portland Ave. So., Bloomington, Minn. 55420.

Grosse Pointe, Mich. *Writing Assessment.* Roger McCaig, Grosse Pointe Public Schools, Grosse Pointe, Mich. 48230.

Honolulu, Hawaii. *Writing Assessment Project.* Dr. Richard Nakamura, Hawaii Department of Education, Communicative Arts Section, Box 2360, Honolulu, Hawaii 96804.

Hazelwood, Mo. *Instructional Management System To Teach Writing.* Connie Gifford, Hazelwood Schools, Florissant, Mo. 63031.

Modesto, Calif. *Modesto Writing Assessment.* Director of Curriculum, Bay Area Writing Project, Modesto City Schools, Modesto, Calif. 95351.

Santa Barbara, Calif. *Holistic Scoring.* Pauline Paulin, Ph.D., Santa Barbara High School, Santa Barbara, Calif. 93100.

Tamalpass, Calif. *Holistic Scoring.* Katherine Blickhahn, Tamalpass High School District, Larkspur, Calif. 94939.

Gainesville, Fla. *Writing Assessment.* Nancy Dean, P. K. Yonge Laboratory School, University of Florida, Gainesville, Fla. 32611.

TESTS TO MEASURE ATTITUDES TOWARD WRITING

Listed below are validated instruments for assessing attitude toward writing. Each measure is described briefly and identified as to its source.

Daly, J. A., and Miller, M. D. *Daly-Miller Writing Apprehension Scale.* A Likert-type scale to measure apprehension and anxiety about writing. John A. Daly, Department of Speech Communication, University of Texas at Austin, 78712.

Emig, J., and King, B. *Emig-King Writing Attitude Scale for Teachers; Emig-King Writing Attitude Scale for Students.* Two scales to measure attitudes toward writing and changes in attitudes toward writing. Barbara King, Douglass College, Rutgers University, New Brunswick, N.J. 08903.

Gere, A. R.; Schuessler, B. F.; and Abbott, R. D. *Attitudes Toward Instruction in Writing.* Measures teachers' attitudes toward importance of standard English, importance of defining and evaluating writing tasks, and importance of student self-expression in writing. Anne R. Gere, Department of English, University of Washington, Seattle 98195.

King, B. *King Construct Scale.* Elicits student and teacher personal constructs concerning writing. Barbara King, Douglass College, Rutgers University, New Brunswick, N.J. 08903.

85